Wakefield Press

The Writing's on the Wall

Bronwen Webb has had a long association with the healthcare sector, including at the Royal Adelaide Hospital, the Queen Victoria Hospital, Flinders Medical Centre and Ashford Hospital. In 1998, she moved from Ashford to the University of South Australia, retiring from the position of Division Director, Division of Health Sciences, in 2013. From 2016, she has worked as a volunteer at the RAH in the Wellness Centre.

Bron has self-published a novel for children, *The Legend of Wild Horse Beach*, and had several short stories published.

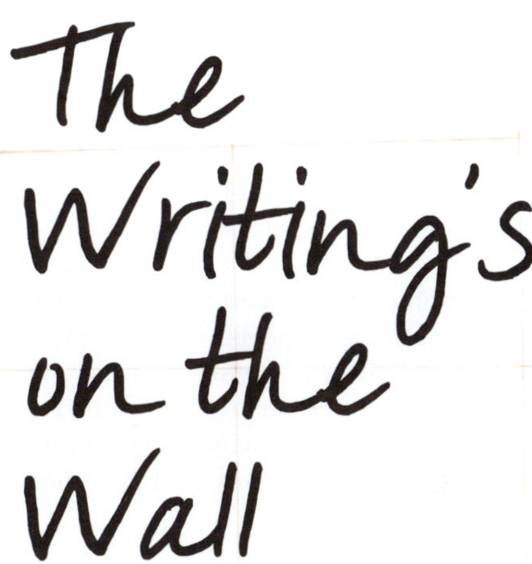

The Writing's on the Wall

Stories, poems and memories by past and present staff and volunteers of the old Royal Adelaide Hospital

Edited by
BRONWEN WEBB

Photographs by Alex Frayne

Wakefield Press

Wakefield Press
16 Rose Street
Mile End
South Australia 5031
www.wakefieldpress.com.au

First published 2018

Authors' names, or a requested nom-de-plume, are published with permission. Names of people who posted goodbye notes on the last day are not published. To protect privacy, names of staff and patients mentioned in stories and poems are either changed or an initial is used. Again to protect privacy, names mentioned in goodbye notes are either not published (including initials if identifiable) or a non-identifiable initial is used.

Goodbye notes have been edited for spelling and grammar and may not therefore look exactly as originally written.

Cover designed by Liz Nicholson, Wakefield Press
Copy-edited by Julia Beaven, Wakefield Press
Photographs by Alex Frayne
Typeset by Michael Deves, Wakefield Press
Printing and quality control in China by Tingleman Pty Ltd

ISBN 978 1 74305 598 4

A catalogue record for this book is available from the National Library of Australia

The Writing's on the Wall
is dedicated to past, present and future patients,
staff and volunteers of the old and new
Royal Adelaide Hospitals.

Contents

A note from the editor

The Writing's on the Wall is the result of a book project initiated by Susan Cameron while she was Manager of the Wellness Centre at the Royal Adelaide Hospital (RAH). The project was then taken up by Michelle Cripps, Director of the RAH's new Centre for Creative Health. As an ex-RAH staff member and a RAH volunteer, I was thrilled to be asked to compile and edit this eclectic collection of stories and poems from past and present RAH staff and volunteers, with fictional pieces, written by me, linking them together.

Also included are the almost 340 goodbye notes posted on the hospital's walls by staff and volunteers before the old RAH closed its doors forever. Some of the notes are highlighted throughout the anthology; all are listed at the end of the book.

The stories and poems – and the goodbye notes – reveal a strong sense of pride in the service the old RAH provided to the community of South Australia and beyond, and a fondness for an institution which, in many cases, has been a part of the staff member's, or volunteer's, life for decades.

There are stories, poems and notes about last days, first days and student days; about caring and sharing, teams and associations, friendship with colleagues, and places and spaces; and, in particular, they are about saying goodbye to the 'old girl'.

The move to the new RAH has now been achieved and the 'new girl' will develop her own history and memories in the years to come. But the old RAH will never be forgotten by the people who worked there, volunteered there, or were cared for within her walls.

Sincere thanks to Susan, Michelle and the members of the initial editorial committee (Pat Rossi, Lyell Brougham and Charmaine Ostermann) for their input, including creating the initial concept, and to all those who contributed stories and poems. Thanks also to everyone who wrote goodbye notes to the RAH, which are all included herein.

The title for the anthology came from an idea by Joan Durdin, who, as a 96-year-old ex-RAH staff member, a volunteer in the RAH Heritage Office between 1985 and 2016, and author of books on the history of nursing at the RAH, has many of her own RAH memories.

The photos were taken by Alex Frayne of Sputnik Films, who also has a family history of service to the RAH.

The cover was designed by Liz Nicholson.

The support from Wakefield Press has been magnificent, and particular thanks go to editor Julia Beaven.

Congratulations to all involved in producing *The Writing's on the Wall.*

Bronwen Webb, 2018

Days to Remember

SERVIRE AC DOCERE

Monday, 4 September 2017

The last of the autumn leaves blew in through the front door as Louise left for her morning shift at the Royal Adelaide Hospital. So much for spring, she thought. Is Adelaide ever going to warm up? She walked to the car, almost falling over the gardening boots her husband persisted in positioning as hazards around the garden, and rummaged for her keys.

The roads leading to the city were covered with leaves and twigs blown there by the wind during a rough night. Louise hardly noticed the debris, her thoughts constantly interrupting her concentration. This would be her very last nursing shift at the old Royal Adelaide Hospital, and she felt sad and unsettled.

Louise pulled over, turned off the engine and took a deep breath, her stomach churning. She couldn't understand why she felt the way she did. After all, the new RAH looked beautiful and the tour of the new wards had excited her. Except they weren't called 'wards' anymore, she'd forgotten the new word they'd used. Well, the patients will be the same. People who need the expert help the RAH could give them.

I'll soon get used to it, Louise thought, and re-started the car. I did so once, and I can do it again. I'm sure all the staff are struggling with their emotions and re-living old memories, just like me.

Louise, now in Adelaide, parked the car, crossed North Terrace and walked briskly towards the RAH, glad of the little touch of warmth the sun was now providing. She entered reception and headed for the escalator and by the time she reached her ward, the rest of the morning shift was arriving. Louise said hello to those she knew. She enjoyed this time of greetings before the handover began. Friendships made during her time at the RAH had lasted many years and she was sure many would last even after they had retired.

Everyone looked a little shell-shocked, tired but excited. And there were some red eyes. So I'm not the only one feeling emotional about saying goodbye, Louise thought.

Tom, the nursing student on placement, rushed into the ward. 'Sorry, Louise,' he said, as he bumped into her. Then, to no one in particular, 'Hey, have you seen them?'

'Seen what?'

'The goodbye messages. There are post-it notes downstairs. I had a look as I came in.'

It was decided they would all take a look when they could, and add their own memory or message. When Louise read them during her morning break, some of the notes brought back memories of her first day at the RAH, twenty years ago. She had been quite terrified, but had been warmly welcomed, and soon settled in and made friends.

I loved you from the moment
I laid eyes on you.

Working at the hospital as a student has helped me to grow into a better health professional, and built me up for my career. Goodbye RAH!

I remember 14/11/77, my first day at the RAH, when I was taken, as a lowly base-grade physiotherapist, to be personally welcomed by the hospital administrator. Times have certainly changed.

First shift I got locked in the stairwell banging on the door until someone came to my rescue. Very embarrassed!

The first day I arrived at the RAH was in 1961. My mother was in Hope ward with women's issues and walked out with a baby. It was a surprise for my mother and my family didn't know she was pregnant, nor is the old RAH a maternity hospital. Years later I came back to the old RAH to see the era out and the new chapter begin at the new RAH.

My first day at the RAH was as a third-year physiotherapy student. I was so impressed by ICU and all the staff here . . . I knew straight away it was exactly where I wanted to work.

A lasting memory of mine would definitely be the hand-drawn map of the hospital I received on my first day. It was terrible, and I got lost multiple times in the first couple of weeks. I am ready for the new maze.

Never a Dull Moment!

Dalia Dunstan

I remember . . .

a plague of fleas in the Emergency Department;

a body missing from the mortuary (an undertaker had collected the wrong one);

being bitten on the hand by a patient on the day I got engaged. Had to have a tetanus injection before I could go to my party;

fire alarms and handsome firemen;

a settee thrown through a window of the Resident Medical Officers' quarters landed on a consultant's Jag;

pink cellophane in the ward lights at Xmas. A consultant thought he'd had a retinal bleed;

a scary night 'specialling' a patient who said he could stop his heart at will;

my roommate babbling about sodium bicarbonate mouthwashes in her sleep;

the porridge at Northfield wards. Best I ever tasted;

being required to cook supper for the night staff at Magill wards. I had never cooked before;

an RMO being chased by a patient on crutches;

waiting with heart in mouth outside night matron's room for my night duty allocation.

Fond Memories

Rhonda Perriam

I have fond memories of being a trainee nurse in the mid-sixties at the old Royal Adelaide Hospital, despite the physical demands over 48 hours, six days a week and all lectures being in one's own time (even waking from sleep when on night duty to attend lectures).

As a first-year trainee, I remember having to collect the ward's linen supply from the laundry building at the rear of the 'new' East Wing. This meant wheeling a large empty wicker basket (which had one small wheel at the front and two larger wheels each side of the basket) down the narrow roadway between the Botanic Gardens and the East Wing. It was downhill all the way and I loved flying along perched on the empty basket feeling as free as the birds in the trees along the fence-line. Coming back with it full of clean laundry was a different story. It must have weighed a ton, but it didn't matter – it was my task to get the linen to the ward.

Another time, when a dear friend's mother died, I remember going to Matron and asking for a morning off to attend the funeral. Asking for time off, or even having a sick day, required a detailed explanation and *always* a doctor's certificate; taking a 'sickie' was risking dismissal or worse! Anyway, Matron looked down at me as I stood in front of her desk and said,

'No, nurse . . . you cannot have the time off; your place is with the living, not with the dead!' Needless to say, I did not attend my friend's mother's funeral.

It was also strict policy in those times that if a nurse married then she would have to resign; several of my friends did marry and regrettably were unable to complete their training.

I trained and lived here 30-odd years ago. So much history for me here! Sad to say goodbye. My mother and half my family trained here.

Heady Days

Annie Windsor (nee Young)

I can't help but smile as I look back at the memories and friendships forged when I embarked on my journey to become a nurse.

In 1950 I completed my secondary schooling, matriculating in Year 11 at Adelaide Girls' High School, which was then in Grote Street. I was sixteen. Nursing was not an option until the age of 18 years. So, what to do during the time in between?

I tried making shoulder pads for a business in Salisbury. It was not really to my liking, not stimulating enough. I then noticed an advertisement from the RAH Blood Transfusion Service (colloquially known as RESUS) calling for technical assistants. Aha! I thought, this should provide me with some background experience for nursing.

I worked weekdays from 9 am until 5 pm, taking blood, sitting alongside the donor and rotating the collecting bottle to stop the blood from coagulating, testing and matching blood to inpatients, and setting up blood transfusions in wards. Another important task was sterilising cannulas, rubber tubing etc in water sterilisers.

Many friendships were forged at RESUS within our special cohort of ten, and we all moved into nursing at the RAH in 1952. We studied and played together as a group. Some of the activities I fondly recall are of playing softball on Saturday afternoons in Rymill Park for the Nurses' Softball Team, being involved in a revue at the RAH, and going on the Gulf trip on the MV *Karatta*, visiting ports of Port Lincoln, Whyalla, Port Augusta and Port Adelaide.

On another occasion, we put our bicycles on the train and travelled to Renmark where we hired a shack on the banks of the Murray River near the Paringa Bridge. We had amazing fun in a rowboat on the river.

Back in those heady days, we all joined the union, the same union representing the boilermakers and firemen.

In our own time we attended lectures on anatomy and physiology and other medical subjects. The lectures were held at the School of Mines on North Terrace, where I also attended an invalid cookery course, learning to make custards, white sauces and such.

I worked different shifts; the ones I recall most clearly were the split shifts 6 to 10 am and 6 to 10 pm, as well as night shifts. Trainee nurses were required to live in, and I did so in various locations. I lived at Eden Park (Kensington), which in my time was for night nurse accommodation. I was collected from there by coach at 10 pm and taken to the RAH, then returned by coach in the morning.

I also lived in Ayers House, annexes on North Terrace between Ayers House and the Botanic Hotel, and the 'new' Nurses Home on Frome Road, where the doors were locked at midnight. Each trainee had a room to themselves with a bed, wardrobe, desk and chair – but no en-suite! We nurses shared a bathroom. Those living on the ground floor left windows open so they could climb through when missing curfew!

As junior nurses we were required each morning to scrub out the metal bedpans and bottles (there were no plastic items in those days) and to test patient urine samples. As there was no central autoclave we also sterilised surgical instruments and set up our own instrument trays.

There were many times I rode pillion on my boyfriend's (now husband) motorbike, to and from duty. When speeding one day, he caught the attention of the constabulary. My boyfriend explained that I was a nurse at the RAH and was late for duty. Thankfully the response was 'OK, on your way, mate'.

I recall being woken by the earthquake of 1954 when living in Ayers House. I turned on the radio to 5KA to find out what had happened.

When we lived in, all of our meals were supplied in a large dining area, and we shared meal breaks. Meals for patients were delivered from a central kitchen to the wards in large containers on a trolley. Ward sisters or staff nurses served the meals onto plates. Nurses then delivered them to the patients and fed the patient if needed.

I remember wards being overcrowded, and less acute patients slept in beds on balconies. Post-operative patients returned to wards for recovery and, on occasion, male patients were very amorous when recovering from anaesthetic! During the Queen's visit in 1954, patients in beds were wheeled to a viewing area on North Terrace balconies. Ambulant patients were taken to the roadside.

Christmas was also a festive time and we decorated the wards, to comfort the patients about having to be in hospital over the festive season. Trainee nurses were lucky to get Christmas Day off.

Matron was very strict and ward sisters made sure their nurses kept the wards looking spick-and-span for the ward round each morning. Linen fresh from the laundry was delivered to the wards. We nurses had to place the sheets and other items in the linen cupboards in exactly the same order for every sheet and pillowcase, with no loose ends to the front. Pillowcases on pillows had to be placed on the patient's bed so that the opening did not face the main ward entry door. These habits were so entrenched that sixty-five years later I still do this in my own home!

We worked six days a week, including weekends and all public holidays. The camaraderie experienced in those times was wonderful, and on 14 December 1955 I graduated after completing my training at the RAH.

I started on 1/10/79 as a Trainee Enrolled Nurse. A couple of years doing a 6 month Orthopaedic Emergency Nursing Certificate. Working in theatre I have scrubbed for operations but also my experience has seen me work as the plaster room nurse, a hyperbaric nurse and much more. I've also done an anaesthetic certificate.

From past memories of a dental nurse training under the RAH banner in 1970s–1990s to a receptionist working in outpatients years later. Wonderful memories, and two lifetimes of career paths.

I recall ward rounds as a med student in Light and Flinders. Moved into the new North Wing as an intern in 1970. That to me was the new RAH!

Early years as a medical student learning the ropes.

Pranks

Lester Phillips

I was a third-year student nurse, and we had Preliminary Training School (PTS) nursing students on our ward. The PTS students were eager to learn and do anything to help senior staff, so this day I sent two of them to collect some vital equipment I needed. With strict and careful instructions, I asked them to go to the Central Sterile Supply Department and collect two packets of Fallopian Tubes and bring them back to me (in the mean time I had teed it up with CSSD). After a few minutes, these eager students returned with my two packets marked 'fallopian tubes' and, prior to opening them, one student asked if they were special instruments. I asked them: 'What do you think?'

It took a while, but then the penny dropped. They had been pranked.

Blushes

Lester Phillips

I trained back in the seventies, one of the few men training to be a nurse. In one of our practical sessions on the wards we had to assist a doctor with a procedure. All I had to do was concentrate and hold the specimen container. My tutor was alongside me and reassured me by saying, 'Just concentrate, I will be here with you.' All was well. I was concentrating as instructed, but then looked over at my female tutor, who said, 'You have the most beautiful blue eyes.'

Well, I lost concentration, my hand shook, and I could feel myself blushing, but I managed to keep the doctor happy and we finished the procedure. Oh, how I loved my training days, the good old days at the RAH.

Verandas, the Botanic, and Northfield

Sally Prior

During my nursing training, some of the older RAH buildings had verandas which were used as ward overflow areas. Mostly the beds on the verandas were allocated to younger patients, as the conditions were fairly basic.

If a veranda was filled with young, male orthopaedic patients, as was often the case, it was a boisterous place, where nurses walked a gauntlet of high-spirited young men who had often been strung up in traction for some time. You could almost smell the testosterone in the air! It made a shift very interesting. If the veranda was empty, we sometimes started a night with fewer patients than we had in the morning. Homeless men living in the Botanic Gardens somehow knew there was a bed on offer, and during the night we would find them curled up in their temporary bed. Unknown to our nursing supervisors, we'd let them sleep and give them breakfast in the morning.

The Botanic Hotel, on the corner of North and East Terraces, was a bit of a watering hole for off-duty staff. One of my memories of the Botanic was sitting there having a drink with friends and hearing about the assassination of Bobby Kennedy. It was also one of the places we'd go looking if a patient were missing. Many a time I headed across North Terrace and helped a patient back to the hospital, drip, catheter, drain and all. 'I was only having one little drink, nurse.'

We did a stint at the Northfield wards of the hospital during our training. Northfield was for infectious diseases, but also had medical patients. It held memories for me because it was to Northfield that I was taken in the early 1950s when I contracted poliomyelitis as a very young child. As a student nurse almost twenty years later, I was allocated to the same ward I had been in as a child. Here, patients needing long-term ventilation were nursed (for post-polio paralysis, or other conditions such as muscular dystrophy). It brought back vivid and scary memories of the ward, where, at that time, children and adults were nursed together. Polio patients were often put in the box respirators overnight, and I remembered lying in my bed listening to the whooshing noise of these machines and being terrified that I, too, would be put in one. All those years later, I realised how very lucky I had been not to be left with the same outcome as the patients I was nursing.

Student nurses on night duty at Northfield were rostered to wake up the staff on an early shift. At 6 am the wake-up call rostered nurse made her way to the nurses' quarters and then went from door to door. If nurses were on an early shift they usually put a 'please wake me' notice on their door, often with detailed instructions on how to achieve that task. That might include coming into the nurse's unlocked bedroom and violently shaking her. I found even that didn't work on occasions! But I woke everyone effortlessly one morning, even those not on early shift. The building was dark and my torch had winked out so I had to feel about for the light switch. I found what I thought was the switch, and pushed it.

It was the fire alarm.

*Making the patient smile even though they're in pain.
It melts my heart that the little joke I have can make them happy.*

Pink Checks and Glad Rags

Annie Windsor (nee Young)

Being a trainee nurse at the Royal Adelaide Hospital in the fifties was both exciting and daunting. Getting used to the discipline and attention to detail at times seemed insurmountable.

We were expected to keep our pink check dresses with their heavily starched collars, cuffs and aprons spotless at all times. As you can imagine, this was not always easy to do! We also spent time perfecting the use of hair clips to keep our 'ice-cream-cone' hats on our heads and at just the right angle. Thankfully the central laundry laundered our uniforms for us. We wore a navy cape for protection and warmth while moving between buildings and wards.

To complete our uniform, we wore black lisle stockings with a central back seam (possibly purchased from John Martins department store). We laundered the lisle stockings ourselves and would hang them to dry anywhere in our room we could find a suitable spot. We had to mend any 'runs' in our stockings, which inevitably appeared from time to time, and to keep our stockings in place, we wore a suspender belt! We wore black lace-up duty shoes (from Clarks Shoe Store).

While on duty, we were given a forty-five-minute meal break. The meals were served in a large central dining room and we had the same menu as the patients. If you were late going to your meal break because the ward was busy (as was usually the case), you were still expected back on time, so we had quite a few 'gulped' meals, no doubt not good for the digestion.

We became accustomed to night shift, and the spectre of Night Matron making a surprise visit and finding something not to her expectations helped us to stay wide awake. There were usually only two nurses in each ward for night duty. The poor patients were awoken at any time from 2 am to 6 am, depending how busy the ward was as all 'bed baths' had to be completed by 6 am. Patient dentures were placed in cups or glasses of water overnight and cleaned by nurses each morning. And as morning approached, the senior nurse had to write the night report in readiness for handover to the day staff, who came on duty at 6 am.

Nurses were required to take patient observations twice a day. Each nurse possessed a beautiful nurse's watch (purchased at our own expense), which had to have a clearly defined second hand. Using our nurse's watches, we checked the wrist pulse point and counted for fifteen seconds, then multiplied that figure by four to give a reading per minute. Respirations were counted in the same way. A normal pulse rate was seventy-two to eighty beats per minute and the respiration rate was twenty per minute. To take a patient's temperature, a mercury glass thermometer was placed under the patient's tongue (or armpit) and the temperature duly recorded in the patient's notes.

When a patient passed away, it was the responsibility of the nursing staff to prepare the body for transfer to the mortuary. This was a huge shock for some of the young nurses who could not face the prospect of 'laying out' the patient. They resigned to pursue other careers. Those of us who continued with our nursing careers gradually accepted these duties as routine.

On the discharge or death of a patient, nurses were required to strip the beds of all linen, wash down thoroughly with disinfectant the wrought iron bedstead on steel castors, the rubber draw sheet, rubber-covered mattress and the metal bedside locker. On completion of this task, we then remade the bed, with very precise 'hospital corners' on sheets, blankets and coverlets.

I spent some time nursing at Northfield Infectious Diseases Hospital in the early 1950s. My nursing duties at that time were mainly with patients who had contracted poliomyelitis, which had reached epidemic proportions. (Poliomyelitis caused various degrees of paralysis in its victims and many either died from the disease or faced wearing leg or arm irons and years of rehabilitation.) Some of these poor patients were so severely affected that they spent their days in huge respirators, known as iron lungs, with just their head protruding.

However, there were also many happy times and we had a good social life, particularly in our graduation year, as most of us celebrated our twenty-first birthdays at this time. We attended many twenty-first parties, usually held at our parents' homes.

Most of my graduation group married their ever-patient boyfriends, who always had to wait for us to get off duty and change into our 'glad rags' before venturing out. Of course, there were many engagements and parties as well – eventually leading to many weddings to attend. Two of my bridesmaids were from the group I trained with over the three years. Friendships continued until well after we had children.

As our children entered primary schooling, most of us considered returning to our nursing careers. I went to the newly opened Lyell McEwin Hospital at Elizabeth as a 'sister'.

Sadly, over the years our friendship circle diminished as we all went our different ways, including to careers overseas. Even more sadly, some of our group have now passed away.

As we have aged, most of us have experienced severe back problems. This has possibly occurred because of the cumbersome duties we performed, such as lifting, handling and rolling some very large and heavy bedridden patients who needed their sheets changed and their backs washed and then rubbed with methylated spirits (they loved that!), and then sitting them up in bed.

As I remember, there were orderlies or wardsmen who kept the floors clean and did other duties, but we were unable to ask them for help!

Fortunately, today's nurses have many support options available to minimise such injuries.

With the passing of the years, many memories fade into the background, so reminiscing about my years as a trainee nurse has revived wonderful memories of a time forgotten.

Following the Footsteps

Anthea Stretton (nee Duffield)

After not enjoying matriculation in high school and giving it much thought I decided to follow in the footsteps of my two older sisters. Hence, I was accepted to start my three year and one month nurse's training at the Royal Adelaide Hospital in 1970, in Group 706, the last intake for that year. Exactly twenty years later the last hospital-trained nurses commenced their three-year training, qualifying in 1993.

There was an initial visit to Rich's Uniforms (made-to-measure specialists in commercial, industrial, nurses' and sisters' uniforms) of 178 Rundle Street Adelaide for a fitting. The completed pink-and-white cotton regulation dresses (no aprons or detachable collars/cuffs now) with white detachable buttons and shanks hidden behind the front double opening of the dress, along with the red RAH pure wool cape, were sent to my parent's house wrapped in brown paper and string. There were black thick stockings (a black texta handy to colour the legs if there was a visible hole in the stocking) and lace-up shoes to complete the uniform. The dresses had to be labelled with your name, as they were laundered, starched and ironed on-site.

I moved into the Eleanor Harrald Nurse's Home, with its large old communal toiletry areas, little kitchenettes and common room. The kitchenettes were supplied with bread, butter, jam, Vegemite, milk, tea and coffee. After living on a farm for most of my life, I still remember looking out the window of my bedroom (consisting of a bed, cupboard and a desk) and seeing only another red brick wall, and feeling very homesick for the open paddock landscape of my family home. Later I moved into the newly built twelve-storey residential wing for a short time, before going to share a house with my sister and her friend until the end of my training.

My training started with a three-month probationary period, after which we were to wear the ice-cream-cone hats. These were later abolished as part of the uniform; they were very hard to keep in place especially if your hair was long and had to be somehow secured into it. Training was divided into four blocks a year and all the theory and practicals were learnt before we were let out onto the wards to practise our new skills.

After each year was completed, a chevron had to be sewn onto the left sleeve of the dress, the same side as your name badge with a nurse's fob watch.

We worked eight-hour shifts, five days a week, on a roster system interspaced with night duty over a set number of weeks per year. It wasn't uncommon to work for ten days just to get four days off duty. Meal breaks of half an hour meant that you could buy a reasonably priced nutritious meal in the staff dining room, but because you only had a short time to get there from wherever you were working, you learnt to hurriedly consume it. This habit, of eating too quickly, I kept for many years.

Sterilisation of most dressing trays, instruments and some

dressings was done on-site with the autoclave system. All was secured in the appropriate-sized bag with tape that changed colour once sterilised. Bandages were sent off to be washed and the nurses in their spare time would re-roll, package and send them off to be autoclaved. Bedpans, made of metal, were ideally warmed before being used. Once used they were covered with a paper cover and placed into the pan steriliser, which always seemed so noisy, especially on night duty.

The 'no lift policy' had not been implemented at that time so to move a patient, nurses were taught the shoulder lift and to use the wind-up lifter with the slings attached to the lifter arm by chains.

Injections were given with disposable syringes and blood pressures were taken manually.

On the days that doctors made ward rounds, all hygiene attendance was to be completed beforehand, with beds made and the opening on the pillow slips facing away from view. All bed linen and towels were white and cleaned/sterilised by the Central Linen Service (and those lovely white sheets were perfect to cover Christmas tables).

During my training I was sent to the Adelaide Children's Hospital for a six-month placement, and to the Infectious Diseases Hospital at Northfield where I saw my first iron lung machine in use.

My graduation ceremony, after qualifying with a gold medal, was held in the Bonython Hall in the grounds of the University of Adelaide where, because seats were limited, only two guests from your family/friends were invited.

Nursing to me has been such a rewarding career. While over the years I have left it to pursue other avenues of employment, I have always returned. I am sure that good basic nursing care instilled in those formative years has meant that the residents I now nurse are being well cared for.

Training in the 60s

Jenny Wallace (nee Duffield)

In September 1963 in Austral House (now Ayers House), PTS Group 636 began their three-month Preliminary Training to become nurses. Most of us were eighteen; all female. While there were no male nursing trainees in the mid 1960s, a few were starting by the time we finished. We attended lectures in the room on the left at the front of Ayers House, learnt practical skills in the room in the middle at the front, and in the ballroom on the right we had keep-fit classes. Those who lived well out of the city area were lucky to be able to sleep in the upstairs bedrooms. A home sister, who lived downstairs, tried to ensure we kept recommended hours!

After officially becoming first years, we were all required to live-in. There were two nurses homes on Frome Road, with reception, switchboard and mail-office in the Eleanor Harrald. The Margaret Graham Nurses Home was next door. There was access to the roof and I can remember sunbathing up there! The dining room for nursing staff was on the ground floor and considering we only had half an hour for meals and many wards were some distance away, this was the time we gave up taking sugar in tea because it took too long having it passed from the other end of the long tables. The 'swimming pool' in the basement was never used as such, instead many of our lectures were held there!

Each ward was staffed by trainee nurses, with a charge sister and a second-in-charge staff nurse. Trainees worked forty-eight hours a week. Daytime shifts were either an 'early' (7 am–3.30 pm), a 'late' (1 pm–9.30 pm), or a 'split-shift' (7 am–12.30 pm and back from 5 pm–7.30 pm). In a surgical ward, all shared in sponging the patients.

Third years were also responsible for many patient observations and the drug rounds – dispensing prescribed patient medicines as ordered, while second years cared for patients' wounds, often re-dressing them twice a day. We made our own dressings and swabs and, having packed them into individual bags, took them, along with other items, to CSSD for sterilising, and later collected them for our use. There were no pre-sterilised, single-use items. Injection syringes and needles were reused many times with the needles kept in a sterilising solution in the ward ready for use.

First years were also responsible for the patients' pressure-area care, and helping to sit them up ready for meals (served from the trolley by the charge sister) and, if necessary, helping feed them. That is when they weren't bedpan cleaning and sterilising in the hot, steamy utility room. Everyone was responsible for writing up patient case notes and for taking part in patient handover for the next shift. By 9 am each day, all patients were to have been sponged and their beds made with neat envelope corners, especially on ward round days when one of the ward's honorary doctors, along with their registrars, RMOs and medical students, would tour the ward to check on each patient's progress, as well as for teaching purposes.

Each year we did three months night duty, working 9 pm–7.30 am and sleeping in the quiet of Eden Park, in Kensington, or at home if preferable. As all lectures and study were in our own time, we would have to hang around after working all night for a 9 am lecture, or try to get enough sleep and be back at the hospital again for a 4.30 pm repeated lecture, given by both tutor sisters and medical staff.

And each year we spent three months away from the North Terrace RAH to work at Magill Aged Care Wards, at Northfield Infectious Diseases Wards (there was still one patient being nursed in an iron lung) or the Paraplegic Centre next door, and lastly to the Adelaide Children's Hospital. And yes, we still needed to come into the RAH for our lectures. Among presenting medical conditions, I remember in particular leukaemia and our lack of success in treating most cases, so different to today.

The RAH was a mixture of old and new wards. In the old Light Ward (male medical) there were thirty patients along both walls and out along the balcony. We lifted and moved portable folding screens to the bedsides for patient privacy. The building close to the East Wing housing Light and Flinders wards, among others, disappeared many years ago.

The new East Wing wards opened in the early 1960s, with vast improvements for patients and staff. Thirty-bed wards contained four bays each with six beds, two double and two single rooms. There was no more lugging screens, instead we used the efficient ceiling-mounted curtains.

Intensive care and cardiac care wards were non-existent when I started my training. An enormous improvement in critical care occurred a few years later when those speciality areas began to evolve. One of many new developments that happened at the RAH!

And so I graduated, gold medal and all. Only two of our group continued at the RAH. After completing my 12-month Staff Nurse period, I was invited to charge ward 5B. Interestingly, this had been my first-ever ward as a trainee and now I was in charge! I needed to ensure best practice care for patients, manage staff, be there to counsel upset or bereaved relatives and manage any emergency that should occur – all at the tender age of 22 years. A huge responsibility, but my three-year training enabled me to do it well. What more could one ask?

Caring and Sharing

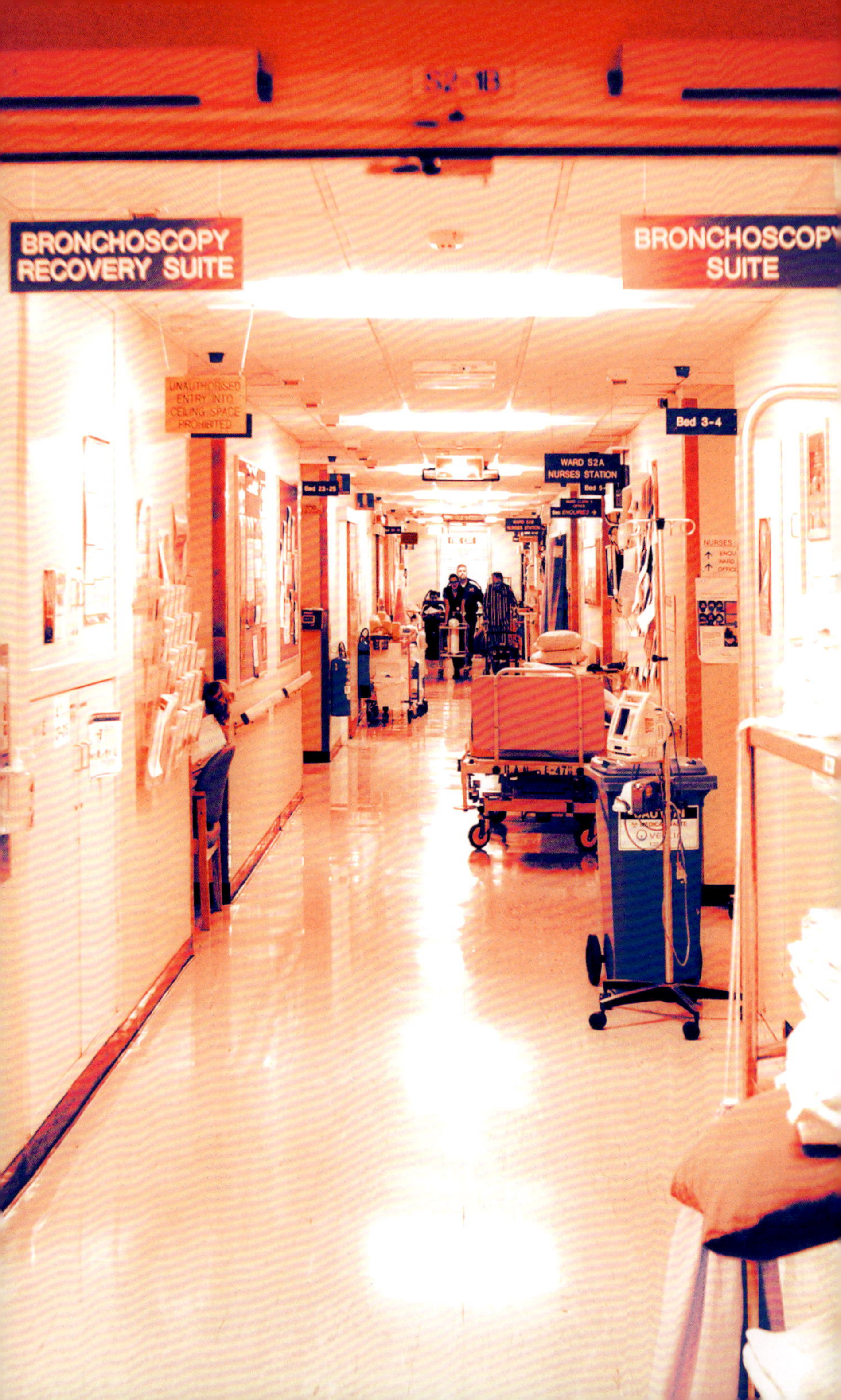
BRONCHOSCOPY
RECOVERY SUITE
BRONCHOSCOPY
SUITE
UNAUTHORISED
ENTRY INTO
CEILING SPACE
PROHIBITED
Bed 3-4
WARD S2A
NURSES STATION

Monday, 4 September 2017

Dennis and Laura sat in the Botanic Gardens, enjoying the sound of the birds. They liked to be by the water-lily lake, especially if the lilies were in bloom. In an hour, Dennis would see the surgeon to discuss the possibility of surgery. It seemed the chemotherapy might not be enough.

The Botanic Gardens had been their place to wait before Dennis's chemotherapy sessions, which had finished a month earlier. They would miss these times in the Gardens if more chemo or radiation therapy were necessary after the surgery. But they'd heard there were many great outdoor places to wait at the new RAH.

After Dennis's diagnosis, the RAH Cancer Centre had made things easier than they had expected. He had dreaded chemo, but to his surprise he found he was treated like a VIP at the centre; a warm blanket wrapped around him if needed, attentive nurses and medical staff, and a comfortable chair – all in a friendly, welcoming and reassuring environment. Dennis's wife, Laura, was by his side and he had dictated his memoirs to her while having chemo. It was therapeutic for them both, and they laughed over things they hadn't remembered for years.

When it was time to leave for the appointment, they headed up the main path of the Gardens toward the squeaky iron gate that had stood at the entrance for many years. They both remembered coming there with their parents and grandparents as children, and had vivid memories of climbing on the twin lions that stood on either side of the entrance path. Now they brought their own grandchildren to the Gardens.

As they walked into the grounds of the RAH and headed towards the main entrance they saw two of the Cancer Centre staff coming towards them.

'You're looking good, Dennis,' one said. 'Is today your appointment with the surgeon?'

'Yes,' Dennis replied. 'We're heading there now. How's the move going?'

'It's going well. We're ahead of the plan. It looks wonderful down there. I hope you don't need to come back, but if you do, I think you'll like it.'

'It sounds great. Whatever happens, I think I'll go have a look. Well, we'd better hurry or we'll be late,' Dennis said. 'All the best for the rest of the move down the road.'

It's all about the people and the care.

RAH Cancer Centre and Good Sports

Ian Olver, AM

The RAH Cancer Centre was a unique entity in the public system in many ways. We crossed disciplines to provide comprehensive care and brought together medical oncology, haematology, radiation oncology, surgical oncology and palliative care. I like to think, as we remodelled the East Wing floors, that we facilitated patient-centred care by having the haematology and oncology outpatients and Day Centre close to each other, with staff that became familiar faces to those who returned again and again for treatment.

We employed the first data manager in the state system and the research staff and doctors' offices were all co-located to facilitate clinical research. Initially all clinical groups were a bit IT poor but we agreed in our second year to spend our entire equipment budgets on IT infrastructure. This gave us a solid platform on which to build. And then there was the telemedicine centre, which enabled our support of the Northern Territory. But all of that is in the glossy annual reports that we produced to document our progress and recognise the achievements of our staff. The story I want to tell is how grateful the patients and staff were for the visits of sportsmen to cheer up our days.

I guess the most significant brush with sporting fame was with Sir Donald Bradman. Jessie, his wife, was a patient of ours and a great Australian in her own right. She had a gift for engaging with those around her, and when after several years she died many from the Day Centre were surprised to discover in the paper the identity of their fellow patient, the woman who had supported and encouraged them while they were undergoing chemotherapy.

A family friend of the Bradman's, Basil Sellers, generously donated funds for the naming rights to the new oncology Day Centre when the East Wing of the old RAH was renovated. Don agreed to attend the opening (as long as the press didn't) and he spent several hours with us chatting with staff, before he took a few of us who had cared for Jessie to his golf club for lunch. It was a magical day and it underlines the fact that it is the relationships, the special people giving their time to recognise the role of the staff and cheer up the patients, that make the memories of a cancer centre, not just how shiny and new it is.

We had a plaque, of course, but placed it in a frame surrounded by pictures of the opening with Don and others who attended. This hung in the corridor of the Day Chemotherapy Centre (when hanging things on walls to cheer people up was allowed) and was soon joined by framed memorabilia of Don's career that various people donated to enhance the impact of the display. I hope the framed plaque survives.

Don was not the only famous cricketer to visit. West Indies captain Carl Hooper, who had married an Adelaide girl, dropped by one day. He spent time with each patient in the Day Centre. The most memorable was with an elderly Italian woman who spoke no English. When a tall dark athletic stranger sat with her and held her hand you could not wipe the smile off her face. Carl also donated a signed cricket bat so that we could raffle it to buy additional items for patient comfort. Again, we were grateful for the generosity of time and selflessness of a sporting hero.

It wasn't just cricket. A group of players from the Adelaide Crows paid a flying visit and brightened the day of both staff and patients. They may have little idea of the impact such a visit has.

One other memorable sporting visit was not by a person but a trophy. We were visited by none other than the Melbourne Cup, in its secure box with its white-gloved attendant and security detail. It was removed carefully from its case and paraded around the Day Centre. The polished gold cup, worth tens of thousands of dollars in its own right and soon to become the focus of a multi-million-dollar horse race, was worth seeing, but it was the theatre of its handling and the reverence of its attendants that sticks in my memory. Wendy, our Day Centre nurse, had convinced me to don silks loaned by a relative of hers to add to the ambience of the day but it was the Cup that outshone all and captivated the outside world visiting the Cancer Centre, demonstrating to the patients that they were worth the extra effort required to do something beyond the routine to improve their wellbeing.

The sporting pedigree of the RAH Cancer Centre is maybe surprising, but is just one last story to tell from those of us who had the privilege of working at the old RAH.

Visiting Papa Joe

Bronwen Webb

Tory's Papa Joe had been sick for two weeks and was in the Royal Adelaide Hospital. Mum explained that Papa Joe was sick because of something called '*you moan eeah*'. Tory was pretty sure that meant that Papa Joe was moaning a lot because he was sick.

Mum also said that Tory couldn't visit Papa Joe just yet, and this caused all sorts of unhappy butterfly feelings in Tory's tummy. These were particularly uncomfortable when Mum was on the phone, crying. That had happened a lot lately, and it scared Tory.

One day, Mum said Tory could finally visit Papa Joe in the hospital and they'd go this afternoon. She explained it would be the last time they would visit this particular hospital, because Papa Joe was moving to a new one the next day. Tory thought it was funny that the new one had the same name as the old one.

They travelled on the tram from Glenelg and then walked up North Terrace. The hospital was on the corner of the street they usually walked down to visit the zoo. There were people everywhere, and some were eating, so Tory asked if he could have something to eat. The kiosk was just inside the front door of the hospital, and Tory asked for a pie. When he'd finished, Mum headed towards what looked like a stairway to the sky. Tory dug his heels into the floor and refused to move.

'Come on, Tory,' Mum said. 'Papa Joe will be waiting for us.'

'I'm not going on that,' Tory said, shaking his head.

'Why not?' Mum asked. Tory was a climber in playgrounds, so this was unexpected.

'There are clouds up there,' Tory said, earnestly pointing. 'It might be going to Heaven.'

Mum looked to where Tory was pointing. Sure enough, there were clouds up there, round pictures of them on the wall at the back of the escalator. 'They're just pictures, Tory. See, they don't move, so they're not real,' she said. 'The escalator takes us up to level five and then we can get the lift up to Papa Joe's ward. It'll be fun.'

Tory nervously stepped onto the escalator, holding on tight to Mum's hand. It was fun. When they got to the top, he asked Mum to take him down the escalator so they could ride the up one again. Which they did. Twice.

Tory though that everything smelled funny in this place, a bit like the 'products' he wasn't allowed to go near at home when Mum was doing the housework, and Tory wasn't sure he liked it. It was nothing like Papa's Joe's house, which usually smelled like the biscuits and cakes that Granny Maria had baked. Granny Maria was a 'baking expert' according to Papa Joe (and Granny Maria), and Tory often went with her to sell her biscuits and cakes at the church's trading tables.

After a ride in a lift, and a walk down the longest corridor Tory had ever seen, they eventually got to Papa Joe's room. Well, Tory thought it was Papa Joe in the bed, but this person had a mask on his face, with a tube attached to the wall.

Tory wasn't sure what to do. Then the person in the bed laughed and it was Papa Joe's laugh, and that convinced Tory he was in the right place. He gave Papa Joe a hug, and whispered, 'What's that thing on your face, Papa Joe?'

'Oh, it's an oxygen mask, Tory,' Papa Joe said, in a voice all whispery and funny. 'It's because of the pneumonia I've had, and it helps me to breathe. But I hope I won't have to wear it much longer.'

'I hope so, too,' Tory said, in a voice that had gone all whispery and funny, too. 'I love you, Papa Joe.'

'I love you too,' Papa Joe said. 'Hey, guess what? I'm going on a trip in a big ambulance tomorrow, down to the new hospital. When you visit me next, you can look out my window and see the trains!'

A nurse came into Papa Joe's room. 'Hello,' he said to Papa Joe, shaking his hand. 'My name is Peter, and I'm your nurse this afternoon.'

Tory smiled at the nurse, put out his hand, and the nurse shook it. 'My name's Tory,' he said. 'Why are you wearing your watch on your chest?'

The nurse smiled. 'That's so I can keep it away from all the handwashing I do, and so I don't scratch anyone. I can look down and see the time while I check your grandpa's pulse.'

'He's not grandpa, he's Papa Joe,' Tory said.

'That's a great name,' said the nurse. 'Do you want to help me check Papa Joe's pulse?'

Tory placed his fingers where the nurse showed him on Papa

Joe's wrist. He counted the pulse as 500. The nurse counted too, and said 500 was almost right.

'Are you the only nurse looking after Papa Joe?' asked Tory.

'No, there are lots of others,' replied Nurse Peter. 'But not only nurses. There are doctors, physiotherapists, radiographers, pharmacists, and . . .'

'I don't know what those people do,' Tory said, looking puzzled.

'Well, I can explain them if you like, but let's just say they are all in the team that looks after your grandpa, I mean Papa Joe. Along with lots of other people.'

'Yeah, lots of others. Lots of people come to see me,' Papa Joe said, pulling himself up on his pillows, with Nurse Peter's help. 'There's the lady that cleans my room, and the orderly that took me to X-ray, the admin people, and the lady who brings my food to me. Oh, and the volunteers. One of them called in this morning to see if I needed anything. His name was Graham.'

Tory cried 'Wow, Papa Joe, you're famous!' and hopped around the room.

Mum told Tory to 'turn it down', then looked at Papa Joe and said sternly, 'You shouldn't be talking so much, Papa Joe.'

Nurse Peter smiled. 'I think Papa Joe is feeling much better,' he said.

Coming to visit grandparents as a child and riding the big escalator.

Aftermath

Christine Hillingdon

Time slows to crawl pace
the need to sleep –
later
when they turn down the lights
as the day nurses go home
and my mind can focus
on why I'm here.
The bruised ache.
The incision
and the shield;
my plastic armour of protection.

Have I Told You Lately . . .

Robert Hutton

As a singer, songwriter and voice coach I have witnessed the positive impact music and singing have on people's lives and their health. Music has the power to transport us to another place in time or circumstance.

One year, at the old Royal Adelaide Hospital, I was singing in the foyer when a patient asked permission to record, on her mobile, my next song. The song, 'Have I told you lately that I love you', was the perfect song choice for her. She was about to have major surgery and wanted to express her love to her husband and children in Alice Springs.

It was an emotional event and something that I will remember for a lifetime.

Bed 12 Ward 20

Mary Gabb

Every day a group of chattering medical students clattered downstairs, past the entrance to the ward, to attend tutorials in the basement. Eleven-year-old Poppy watched from her bed by the window for their arrival. The temporary pre-fabricated paediatric ward, detached from Auckland hospital, was set on a hill; underneath was a basement used for medical student tutorials.

After a month she had got used to the routine of the ward. Bed baths every day . . . she loved these. Each child was washed from top to toe before ward rounds and sheets were changed daily. To take the pressure off the morning staff, one enthusiastic night nurse gave the day nurses a head start by starting bed sponges at five o'clock in the morning. Not everyone tolerated being woken while it was dark, but Poppy loved the sensuous feeling of being soaped up by torchlight, the crisp clean sheets, then drifting off into luxurious sleep before breakfast. She was the first to be sponged, always clean and fresh by breakfast time. Then came breakfast on trays with ward rounds afterwards. In the 1950s the wards had to be immaculate before the gods descended, otherwise matron would be displeased. No one wanted an irritated matron.

Poppy had quickly learned that her side of the long, twelve-bed ward was occupied by patients whose stay was longer than that of the children in the beds opposite. The six facing beds were occupied by young patients, white plasters applied to various parts of their anatomy supporting broken bones as they mended. Others proudly displayed dressings and stitches resulting from operations of one kind or another – appendix, tonsils and a variety of other complaints. On that side of the ward beds shuttled to and fro from the operating theatre every day. These children were mended after three or four days, then discharged, to be jubilantly reunited with an excited family. The turnover on her side of the ward was much slower; she had now been here a full month.

Poppy was the longest resident of Ward 20. In that time her mother had visited once and so had her father. Before Poppy could see her, she could hear her mother's footsteps approaching along the ward's length. Always in high heels, the quick footsteps of her mother had a unique and familiar ring. Her father came a week or so later, bringing her a florist's bouquet of pink and mauve asters in matching tissue paper, the first flowers she had ever received, and a bar of chocolate! Poppy understood that her parents were unable to visit more frequently, because of the arduous 200-mile car trip.

Dr L. was the consulting paediatrician who attended patients on her side of the ward. On his regular rounds he was accompanied by a constellation of young trainees. He looked at charts at the end of each bed, discussed the patient's problems at length, and required students to make specific examinations, prodding stomachs, flexing joints and testing reflexes. He gave treatment orders before moving to the next bed.

Poppy listened with interest as each patient was discussed. Students hung on every word spoken by this god-like consultant. And so did Poppy! She learned about lumbar punctures and their after-effects. She didn't need one of those, thank goodness. But she did have a '*Man-two*' (Mantoux) test and was told that it was a test for tuberculosis. She couldn't figure that out, when they knew the problem was her painful legs.

On a subsequent visit, Dr L. drew his students away from Poppy's bed. They had a whispered discussion out of earshot of the child. *You should tell me what you are talking about,* thought Poppy! After that, her bed was skipped from the consultant's daily round, and no longer did groups of medical students hover around her bed, ask questions or examine her legs.

The student doctor perched himself at the end of Poppy's bed. He had detached himself from the noisy group of students, and instead of leaving the building with the others, bounced into the ward and made a beeline for her bed.

'Hi, and how are you today, Poppy?' Poppy was overcome with shyness. Then without another word, the young man fished a recorder out of his knapsack and began to play the haunting melody '*Greensleeves*', then quickly broke into the lively '*Sailor's Hornpipe*'. Poppy smiled and clapped.

'I'll be back,' he promised, packing his recorder away. With a grin and a friendly wave to the other children, the visitor disappeared, bounding out of the ward with long athletic steps.

On his next visit, the young doctor removed the stethoscope swinging from his neck and showed Poppy how to use it. She listened to his heart, then to her own, and was fascinated.

'Okay, you can look after it for me and I will come back for it,' he said. Poppy felt proud that she was trusted with this piece of equipment, but she worried – *had he failed an exam, was he quitting doctoring?* In the next few days the stethoscope was given a good workout. Forbidden to walk, Poppy skated around the ward on a bedpan when supervision was slack, and listened to the beat of other children's hearts.

Sally aged ten in the next bed, was a living Snow White with her alabaster skin, raven black hair, and extraordinarily blue lips. Poppy was envious of her porcelain-doll looks, and particularly envied the attention she got from the medical staff. Sometimes she even had blue circles under her eyes. Nurses said she was a *blue baby.* Poppy discovered that Sally had a very different heartbeat from the others that she had heard. It had an extra *'shhhhh'* after the regular *'lub-dub'*. The nurses checked her colour frequently.

When the craft volunteers brought materials for her to make a beanie, Poppy had an idea. She would surprise her favourite visitor. For days she worked diligently on her project, carefully avoiding bloodying it from pricked fingers. When all the pieces were stitched together, she topped it off with a multi-coloured pom-pom. She was pleased with the result.

'Really, for me?' he asked when the child presented him with the gift. 'You are a tricky one. *Bay of Plenty* colours, I see!' Poppy giggled. 'How does it look?' and he paraded around the ward with the beanie on his head.

'Great job – I will wear it to the footie!'

He picked up his stethoscope and slung it around his neck. 'Did you get to do some listening with this? Clever isn't it! Gotta fly now, Poppy, I'm late.' Poppy beamed. *He's not going to quit after all. He will be a great doctor!*

'You'll be leaving us today, Poppy!' said the nurse brightly.

'I will miss you all when I go home . . . this was the best bed. And I don't even know his name,' Poppy whispered.

'Poppy, you are not listening. I didn't say that you were going home!' Poppy noticed that the nurse's face was flushed and she looked troubled. Why was she upset and angry?

'What do you mean?'

'You are going to the Wilson Home. An ambulance will take you there. It's a place where crippled children are looked after.' Her nurse looked worried.

'Oh, it's all right, I don't mind!' Poppy tried to be comforting. 'I've been there before. I was there when I was four . . .'

But the nurse was not listening, something was wrong. Her face was flushed and Poppy thought she was going to cry. Turning on her heel and with head down, she walked quickly back to the nurse's station without another word.

Time passed and Poppy migrated to Australia after training as a teacher. In Adelaide she met and married a medical student, had two daughters and subsequently received multiple joint replacements to deal with the ravages of lifelong juvenile arthritis.

Serving as a lay member of the Royal Adelaide Hospital Research Ethics Committee for a number of years, she was astonished when she realised one of the practising clinicians on the committee was the grandson of the eminent New Zealand paediatrician who had looked after her so long ago in the Auckland Hospital.

The value of human warmth of caring staff was learned early in the course of her childhood hospital experience – and it was never forgotten.

#HelloMyNameIs

Bronwen Webb
(with the permission of Chris Pointon)

#HelloMyNameIs is a Twitter hashtag started in the United Kingdom by the late Dr Kate Granger and her husband, Chris Pointon. It calls upon healthcare staff to introduce themselves to their patients.

Kate was a medical specialist in elderly care and worked in the NHS. In her late twenties she was diagnosed with a particularly nasty cancer and initially given only a few months to live, a diagnosis given after she suffered acute abdominal pain while visiting relatives in the United States. The doctor telling her of her prognosis did not introduce himself, nor make eye contact, leaving her alone and devastated in a hospital cubicle.

This was the beginning of a harrowing time for Kate and Chris over the five years leading up to Kate's death, aged thirty-four, in July 2016, with chemotherapy and other treatments taking up their already busy lives. Kate discovered very early in that time that most health professionals did not introduce themselves. She often felt she was not a person, that she was only seen as her cancer. She also felt she was left out of decision-making at times. If she, as a doctor, felt like this, what was it like for the general population? She talked about this to Chris, who suggested she do something about it.

An amazing campaign began on social media, using the hashtag #HelloMyNameIs, to remind healthcare staff of the importance of introductions to facilitate compassionate care. The campaign and its message has since been taken up by NHS hospitals, as well as others in the UK and overseas, including Australia. Name badges, lanyards, seminars, and conferences have all used the hashtag. Celebrities across the world have had their photos taken holding a poster with the hashtag. Funds poured in to support cancer research and the campaign.

Kate's efforts were rewarded when she received an MBE in the United Kingdom; other awards soon followed. An annual Kate Granger Award for Compassionate Care was launched by the NHS England in 2014. Since Kate's death, Chris has been travelling the world, keeping his promise to Kate that the campaign would continue and grow. It has already surpassed anything Kate and Chris envisaged when it first began (including 1.8 billion impressions on social media), and continues to gain in strength and influence.

So, why is introducing yourself to a patient so important? Kate said it very well.

> *We decided to start a campaign, primarily using social media initially, to encourage and remind healthcare staff about the importance of introductions in healthcare.*
>
> *I firmly believe it is not just about common courtesy, but it runs much deeper. Introductions are about making a human connection between one human being who is suffering and vulnerable, and another human being who wishes to help. They*

> *begin therapeutic relationships and can instantly build trust in difficult circumstances.*
>
> (Hellomynameis.org.uk)

Have you said 'Hello my name is' to your patients today, or had it said to you?

Held hands,
Dried tears,
Laughed, cried,
Saved lives and watched last breaths.

2 years spent with wonderful caring colleagues.
Good times and bad, always a friendly face and kind, caring shoulder to lean on.
Here's to making new memories.

Christmas Day

Chris Bryant

It was Christmas morning and we had had two emergencies so patients had not been washed – and Christmas dinner was about to be served. I was asked to go and wash a patient in the male bay.

I went behind the curtain to a man of about thirty-five. Yes, he could do most of it himself if given a bowl. I said I would come back and wash his back and legs. 'We'll only need to do one leg actually,' he said. When I came back to complete the wash, he told me what happened to his lost leg.

He had finished his shift in Adelaide and, on the spur of the moment, he decided to motorbike to Port Pirie to surprise his family. It was about midnight when he set off with a full moon and clear sky.

Just before Port Pirie there are some low hills and it is here that the accident happened. He did not know what caused him to go over the side of the road. He and the bike went down a steep embankment, hitting a wire fence at the bottom. The wire acted like a saw, severing off his leg. He lay unconscious. Meanwhile two plain-clothes policemen were travelling from Adelaide to Port Pirie. It was 5 am.

Our motorbike rider awoke from his unconscious state, now minus a leg and failing fast. He thought the only way to save himself was to crawl up to the road, where he might be seen by passing cars. The full moon and stars were fading as dawn approached.

Now to those passing cops. The passenger said, 'What's that over there on the bank – looks like a leg.' The driving policeman said, 'Pull the other leg!' But he thought they should do a U-turn and check it out. It was dawn now and they were looking across at what did appear to be a leg on the bank.

The mangled bike was now obvious to them and they heard the rider call for help as he passed in and out of consciousness. They rushed over to him and started giving him CPR. Fortunately, they were near Port Pirie and called for an ambulance.

Just then it got really weird – a cyclist out for morning training came across the scene. But what he saw was two guys apparently assaulting a bloody guy with only one leg. He rode down the road to what he thought was a safe distance away from a 'crime scene'. He used his mobile phone to call the cops to report the mugging. At just the moment he finished the call, an ambulance arrived, with siren blaring and lights flashing. He was amazed at their quick response to his call.

He turned back to investigate, and the real story unfolded. As it happened, the plain-clothes police saved the guy's life. The motorcyclist said it was the best Christmas he had had – he lost a leg but was alive!

Patient Memories

Mel Baker

I have many memories of patients at the RAH, but some remain vivid despite the years, including the following. (Names are changed.)

Jason, who sustained a significant head injury, was transferred to my neurosurgical ward after a long period in intensive care. He was in a vegetative state, but over some months showed subtle signs of hearing and understanding us. We were able to feed him, supplementing the tube feeds he had, and we talked to him as if he could hear us, even though he just looked into the far distance, never at us. Everyone who talked with Jason told him to raise one finger to answer yes to a question, and two fingers for no. For some time, we got no response to this.

One day, Jason's grandmother was feeding him and asked if he'd like some ice cream. Jason raised his forefinger and, when asked again, raised it once more. I'll never forget the excitement of his family and the ward staff. From then on, he consistently and appropriately answered questions, slowly raising one finger for yes and two for no. However, he would never do this when his doctors were at his bedside, and so the doctors teased the nursing staff for imagining things. Jason, of course, heard this, and stubbornly continued his deafness to questions when the doctors were present.

Eventually, Jason was scheduled to be moved to a nursing home. It was an understandable decision by the medical staff, given they saw no significant improvement in him, but heartbreaking for those of us who had seen Jason's finger talk. I sat by Jason's bedside one day and pleaded with him to show the doctors what he could do. On the next ward round, he still didn't show what he could do. I tried again, this time explaining the consequences of not demonstrating his improvement. On the next ward round Jason complied, and amazed the doctors with his one and two finger answers. The neurosurgical registrar turned to me and said, 'Looks like you were right, Sis, we'd better reassess him.'

Jason was sent to a rehabilitation hospital.

Several years later, a woman approached me in Rundle Mall. She was Jason's mother, and she told me that Jason was living at home and, while still severely disabled, had made a life for himself.

Frank had his leg in a Thomas splint because of a fracture. This meant his leg was strung up in traction with cords and pulleys attached to a frame, which included bars above the bed. Frank was also suffering from the effects of withdrawal from alcohol and really kept us on our toes. One day we found him sitting on the bar above his bed, his leg and Thomas splint dragging on the bed while he contentedly smoked a cigarette. A friend had brought in the cigarette and Frank used it to burn through the splint and traction cords. We managed to safely get him down and 're-strung', among much hilarity from him and all of us.

The patients make this job worthwhile.

A Golden Sunrise

Anthony Lynch

I was rushed
and so I did not tell you
Shall I tell you now?

Last Wednesday as I drove in
I saw
behind the dark outline
of the gentle hills,
a total golden sky
of such even colour
my world and I were bathed.

I knew from where you were
you would be seeing the sunrise, too.
It confirmed that the previous Monday
had been my best day so far.
Thank you for your part in it.

Forever, and whenever I see
a golden sunrise
behind some hills,

I will think of and remember you.

If now from your discharged bed you cannot see
the golden sun rising,
instruct *Fetch a mirror*
Fix it rightly on a strong wall.
Then view 'gainst dark hills
the warm bathing, or
watch the willy-wags
dancing
in the garden.

Convalescing

Christine Hillingdon

I lie
a lady-in-waiting
trying to regain my vitality,
my normality
buried under a drug-induced haze
of what seems like
forever.

I close my good eye
and feel the mark of the scalpel
on the other.
A tear rolls across the reddened surface
gently soothing
the swollen tissue.
'A roadmap,' he had said
and indeed, I could relate to the tyre marks.

Training at the RAH back in the 80s and living in the residential wing with all the girls on level 5. . . best 3 years of my career. Being part of the retrieval service MEDIFLIGHT for 12 years was physically demanding but so rewarding.

Maggots and MET calls.
Morphine and mayhem.
Laughter, friendship, family.
15 years of excellence and commitment.
Mending wounds and hearts.
Helping people to live and die with dignity.

Teaching spinal patients at the Hampstead how to paint. And get them to sing karaoke. I was as orderly there (30 years ago).

Reflections on Critical Care at the RAH 1946–1974

Heather Schubert (nee Duffield), OAM

'You are nothing unless you know from where you came.'
– an old Maori saying.

During my nursing career it has been my good fortune to be involved in the birth of post-operative recovery and Intensive/Coronary Care Units at the RAH.

Prior to 1946, patients had been returned to their wards as soon as they woke from their anaesthetic – sometimes resulting in deterioration occurring during transport, with life-threatening results. A longer period of observation was required before transfer.

The McEwin Building was built in 1946 with new operating theatres on the ground floor, a post-operative recovery area behind theatres, and two post-operative surgical wards – Coombs and Ritchie – located on the first floor above the theatres. Initially the new recovery area opened for just four hours a day, but this was increased to twenty-four hours a day by 1960 to care for the increasing number of cardiothoracic surgical patients. In 1961, non-surgical patients were admitted to the recovery ward for the first time – twenty-three in that year – a third of these needing care due to barbiturate overdoses. Many needed assisted ventilation with new mechanical ventilators now available for use outside of theatres.

In 1964, my final year as a student nurse, I was sent to work in the recovery area – initially for six weeks – and again later as a staff nurse (first year RN). It was completely different nursing and I gained valuable experience in managing the airway and assessing vital signs in vulnerable post-operative patients.

With the recovery area open fulltime there was a need for increased numbers of nursing staff. Three first year RNs were regularly rostered to work in the area to help meet staffing needs – they worked on day duty for four weeks, and then completed fourteen nights straight on night duty, followed by a much-needed week off! Wouldn't be allowed today, but they coped.

As a staff nurse in the area in 1965, I vividly remember my two weeks night duty as the only RN on duty with a student nurse – we had varying numbers of patients requiring assisted ventilation, airway management, good nursing care, IV infusions and some cardiac monitoring. It was a steep learning curve with only the anaesthetic registrar, usually asleep in a nearby room, as back-up. We learnt to take responsibility very quickly!

I remember admitting a twelve-year-old girl who had been hit by a bus and was found to have a severe C2 spinal cord injury – dealing with a grieving family for the first time after they had been told she would not survive was challenging. Despite this experience, I requested to return to the area after completing my twelve months as a staff nurse, and so began my sojourn into Intensive Care. To say this was an exciting & challenging time to be nursing is an understatement!

Assisted ventilation of patients was also changing. During a polio epidemic in 1937 in Australia and overseas, the South Australian Both brothers (early biomedical engineers) were asked by the SA Government to design a cheaper version of the iron lung being used in the UK. The new apparatus was used at RAH Northfield Infectious Diseases Hospital where polio victims were cared for – and later also used in the UK.

I remember working in the Northfield Infectious Diseases Hospital as a student nurse in 1963 and being allocated to the ward caring for polio patients – thus caring for those in the iron lung. It was a scary experience knowing the patients in the big tank-like apparatus were unable to breathe for long when the tank was opened (to allow for basic nursing care) or if someone switched off or disconnected the power that kept the tank pressure fluctuating to push and pull air in or out of the patient's lungs.

In the 1940–1950s endotracheal intubation with red rubber ET tubes (ETT) facilitated airway management and permitted more effective use of assisted ventilation during surgical procedures. They were not required for the patients in the iron lung. During 1957–1962 nine tetanus patients were managed by paralysis, intubation and assisted ventilation in a special 'Quiet Room' at the RAH – with one anaesthetist present at all times. Records show that a nurse was also rostered to provide basic nursing care.

Patients were paralysed with drugs and hand ventilated via bag to endotracheal tube by shifts of medical students. This presented huge logistical problems with lack of staff and prompted an increase in staff numbers in the developing Department of Anaesthesia, and was the incentive to find a better way to deliver assisted ventilation via mechanical means. Calling on overseas experience and with assistance from a local biomedical equipment company a simple mechanical Bird Respirator was utilised to replace hand ventilation and, as blood-gas analysis was not yet available, there was a degree of guess work involved in setting controls. Red rubber ET tubes were used initially and a tracheostomy performed after two days.

In 1962, Dr Maurice Sando was appointed director of the Anaesthetic/Intensive Care Department and registrars were appointed to assist. By 1963 increasing numbers of non-post surgical patients, requiring increased medical and nursing care, were being admitted to the recovery area. Barbiturate drug overdoses were seen less frequently, but were replaced by patients having experienced major trauma, head and spinal injuries, surgical complications, major respiratory problems, tetanus or neuromuscular disorders.

More knowledge and skill were now needed by both medical and nursing staff working in the recovery area. Both groups learnt new skills on the job – often at the same time – setting the precedent for working together as a team that marked a significant change in doctor–nurse relationships that carried over into ICU/CCU developments during the years ahead.

We nurses became adept at monitoring the ventilated patients, caring for ETTs and providing tracheal suction to maintain airway clearance – and we also had to dismantle and disinfect ventilator tubing and reassemble ready for the next patient. Cardiac monitors became available in the mid 1960s and provided another dimension to nursing.

In the 1950s, the Both brothers not only developed the iron lung, but also produced the world's first direct writing electrocardiograph (ECG) machine, which was subsequently manufactured in the UK. It was the forerunner of ECG machines and cardiac monitors that, by the early 1960s, were available and increasingly utilised to monitor acutely ill patients in both theatres and recovery. With the increasing knowledge of CPR – and use of cardiac monitors and external defibrillators – these became central components of the care and treatment of patients experiencing acute myocardial infarctions (heart attacks) and led to the development of coronary care units.

By 1967 I took over as charge nurse in recovery. The new technology now available – monitors, defibrillators and simple ventilators – meant more sick patients were being cared for in the recovery area and I took on a major role in teaching new staff as nursing numbers increased.

Dr Sando had been awarded a Churchill Scholarship in 1966, to review ICU developments overseas and came back to the RAH with many new ideas to be incorporated into the new operating suite, recovery, and intensive and coronary units planned for the new North Wing building. Over the next few years I worked closely with him to help plan for required nursing staffing, equipment and supplies and provide staff education for the urgently needed new recovery and ICU/CCU areas to be opened in 1969.

In 1969, the first South Australian custom-built combined intensive care and coronary care unit opened in Ward Q4 on the 4th floor of the new North Wing building, with two six-bed areas for ICU plus a separate six-bed area for CCU.

The concept of monitoring patients from the central nursing station in ICU areas required a change in staff organisation – one nurse was required to be present continuously in the nursing stations and a staff-patient ratio of 1:1 or 1:2 was required for patients located in separate cubicles. In addition, we allocated a team leader in each of the two ICU six-bed areas for support of less experienced staff and to help cover during meal breaks. Nursing staff increasingly required further education as they struggled to learn new skills and take on more responsibility for complex patient care. In 1970 a new post-basic intensive/coronary care nursing course was commenced to meet this need.

In 1968 I was sent with another member of the senior nursing staff in recovery to Melbourne. We were to attend the first short coronary care course run by the Royal Melbourne Hospital, which had recently opened one of the early coronary care units in Australia. It was again a steep learning curve, but proved invaluable to our confidence as we absorbed the knowledge required to both teach and work in this area of nursing. On our return to the RAH I continued in charge of McEwin recovery/intensive care area and the other RN took charge of the two-bed Ritchie Annexe (on the floor above recovery) when it opened in early 1969.

The move to the new ICU/CCU meant new equipment,

more sophisticated ventilators and more acutely ill patients, so ongoing education was needed once again. Initially it was provided by senior medical and nursing staff and in late 1969, under the direction of a senior nurse educator from the School of Nursing, the first ICU/CCU course was developed, with a formal education focus and clinical experience rotation for students through ICU, CCU and recovery.

All key senior nursing staff in ICU and CCU (including me) completed the first six-month course in 1969–1970. Later it was extended to twelve months, and conducted by critical care trained RNs. It was renamed the Critical Care Nursing course to reflect the broader base of clinical experience now gained by participants in recovery, ICU, CCU, Cardiothoracic Surgical Unit and the Cardiovascular Investigation Unit.

By the mid-1970s both ICU and CCU were well established, retrieval services were part of the Unit's medical and nursing responsibilities, and senior nursing staff were taking over teaching and management roles. I moved on to spend several years as nursing supervisor of other specialist units being set up on the 4th floor – High Dependency Ward, Burns Unit and Spinal Unit.

In 1980 I moved to the School of Nursing and took over as educator for the Critical Care Nursing course for ten years, before leaving the RAH in 1991.

ROYAL
ADELAIDE
HOSPITAL

EMERGENCY

Colleagues and Teams

S2AL
Q8BL

Tuesday, 5 September 2017

The doors to the RAH Emergency Department opened just after midnight and an ambulance trolley, one of many to come during the night, was pushed in. Paul, the senior ED doctor, and two nurses moved forward to hear a brief handover from the paramedics as they wheeled the trolley into a resuscitation room. Paul had been alerted about the road accident half an hour before, and he and his team had prepared the resuscitation room for its third occupant that night.

The team immediately set about cutting away the patient's damaged clothes so they could more easily assess him. The badly injured young man was unconscious and already intubated, being 'breathed' by a paramedic squeezing a breathing bag.

'Head injury and multiple fractures – and probably some belly stuff; he's pretty bruised there,' Paul said. 'Let's get him assessed and stabilised and then get some X-rays and scans done.'

The team worked through a well-established protocol, and Paul felt pride in how well emergencies were handled in the ED. He'd worked there for four years and loved every minute of it, despite the long, tiring hours and the frequent stressful situations. It was one of many areas at the RAH where skilled teamwork was essential to patient outcomes.

The young man's family had just arrived and were sitting in the waiting area. A volunteer and a nurse tried to calm them with cups of tea and warm blankets to wrap around the patient's girlfriend, who was shaking uncontrollably. Gradually the family settled to anxiously wait for news.

As the night wore on, Paul and his team were thinking of the need to have the department empty by 7 am, in time for the doors to the old RAH's Emergency Department to close, forever, and those of the new RAH Emergency Department to open.

When, just before 7 am, the last emergency patient was discharged, Paul and his team watched them leave and locked the doors.

'That's it, the end of an era,' Paul said. 'A new one has just begun.'

'It's sad, but exciting, too,' said a doctor, her arm around the shoulders of another.

One of the nurses, holding a cricket bat and ball aloft, said, 'Anyone for cricket?' And, at a time when it was normally full of patients, the Emergency Department of the old RAH resounded with the 'whack' of bat and ball.

Lavender Lads and Ladies

Barb McFarlane

Retired from paid work, what can I do
to help the community and be meaningful too?
Lavender Lads and Ladies looking to help;
I'll give it a go, I'm sure I can do
the work they are needing, and proudly I'll wear
the shirt with a lavender hue.

Tried ward rounds and laundry and tea trolley too,
then worked in ED, found a calling so true.
The nurses and doctors continually race,
but as a Lavender Lady, I keep up with the pace,
stocking warm blankets, folders and such,
picking up scripts, walkers and crutch.

Talking to patients and relatives who
need a hug and a cuppa, and a kind word or two.
Being called an angel, as you do what you can
to make their visit a more pleasant one,
leaves you feeling warm as you finish your shift.
So, try it for yourself, you'll get such a lift.

The Lives and Times of RAH Radiographers

Teresa Wong

I am a radiographer,
and in leisure a photographer.
I've been at the RAH for 21 years,
working with my professional peers.

Gone are the days
when unreported X-rays
were put in an unreported packet
and to the doctor the patient went.

Manufacturing of manual X-ray machines decreased.
The introduction of computed radiography increased.
Next, digital radiography came,
and image processing was no longer the same
– almost instant!

Morning coffee is had at the kiosk or Cibo,
lunch at the Exeter, Chopstix or Nano.
The Botanical Gardens is lovely for lunch,
with the past RAH radiographers bunch.

Bus tickets and cards are bought from the newsagent,
lunchtime shopping done at Myer, Kathmandu or Target.
Post-work dinner available at San Giorgio Café,
after-work drinks had at Belgian Beer Café.

Many RAH staff were guilty of jaywalking
prior to installation of the pedestrian crossing.
The new RAH entrance brought Music Matters,
bringing joy to those whose lives were in tatters.

Memorable RAH Radiology things include:
the hospital Christmas BBQ,
the Radiology department move to OPD building,
Radiology's post-party sleep in the Resi Wing,
the C1 Resus Room becoming forlorn,
changing from blue to black radiographers' uniform,
the upgrade of RAH car park to multilevel –
thankfully the new hospital's name will be identical!

A Fellowship Supreme

Claire Colbey

I wait in line at the station, to catch the 7:10,
same thing every morning, here we go again.
The train arrives and on I get, hoping to find a seat,
then off we head, on our way at last, without missing a beat.

People on their mobile phones, playing games and such,
schoolgirls laughing loudly, it's really all too much.
Everyone seems oblivious to everybody else,
too wrapped up in their own world, too absorbed in self.

'Next stop is Adelaide, please mind the gap,'
my book quickly stowed in the bag upon my lap.
At last we enter the station, with a mighty lurch and jolt.
I leap onto the platform, joining the masses as they bolt.

Onto the street we eventually burst, then on to our destinations,
obstacles getting in the way just add to our frustrations.
Finally, I'm there at last, I've walked at quite a pace.
In I go and head towards that old familiar space.

On my way I exchange a nod, or even a word or two,
with people whom I've come to know, people who work there too.
People who engender warmth, especially from their smile,
who always find the time to stop and chat a little while.

A 'family' of sorts, I like to say, people seen most every day,
colleagues who can be relied upon, in every imaginable way.
A team that I am proud to say is one of the very best,
the Royal Adelaide Hospital – a cut above the rest.

Working as an outpatients admin has been a great experience and being in a diverse group of hardworking individuals has been a rewarding journey.

I have laughed many times over the last 28 years. It's been an education in life.

I have been to various hospitals in my working life but always come back to the RAH. It is like coming home in many ways. I trained here, met my wonderful wife here, and have been a patient here. No matter the building, it is the RAH family that matters.

Twin Trouble

Lesley Reed

My identical twin sister and I did our nursing training at the Royal Adelaide Hospital during the early 1960s and were staff nurses and eventually charge nurses at the hospital. My sister started her training about a year after me, having made up her mind about a nursing career later than I did.

In the first few months of training, as a 'black probationer' (or 'black pro' as we were unkindly called) I lived in a prefabricated building in the grounds of Ayers House. This was the first time I'd ever lived away from home and I regularly called my mother on the old coin-operated phone there, threatening to resign from the program while trying to hide my tears from the other student nurses. I'm glad my mother always talked me out of it!

I was absolutely terrified the first time our probationer group was taken to a ward to make beds and wash real patients. The high pace of activity in the ward was very different to practising in the classroom, the nursing and medical staff (and nursing students with stripes) seemed to know so much, and the sister-in-charge was extremely scary. However, I soon realised I loved being with the patients.

My twin sister and I occasionally worked in close proximity, although never on the same ward. We needed to complete a period of time at the Children's Hospital (as it was then) as part of our training and were sent there at the same time. We worked on adjacent wards on the same level of the hospital and caused much confusion. One of those times was when the sister-in-charge of my sister's ward thundered down the corridor towards me, wanting to know why I wasn't in her ward and saying she had noticed me down in the other ward on several occasions. I replied that her ward wasn't my ward, and that I had a twin who worked on her ward. She was very sceptical about this and her anger increased. I had to go looking for my sister and bring her to the sister-in-charge to prove there were two of us.

When I was in third year, and my sister was in second, we were on duty at the same time in the casualty building (the emergency department was called 'casualty' in those days and was on the ground floor of what was in later times the Allied Health building). My sister was working on the first floor in the male orthopaedic ward and I was in casualty on the ground floor. A young man who had been involved in a road accident and seriously injured, was treated in casualty with me assisting the resident medical officer (RMO). The patient was then brought up to my sister's ward, accompanied by the same RMO and a staff nurse. My sister met them at the lift and the RMO gave her a shocked look. 'Gawd, nurse,' he said. 'They really work you hard, don't they?' She had no idea what he meant, but the staff nurse, with a glint in her eye, agreed that they did work me very hard, running up and down the building all shift long. Later that shift, my sister met the RMO again while walking through the X-ray department. He stopped, eyed her suspiciously, and said, 'I suppose you must be the triplet!'

We lived in the Margaret Graham or Eleanor Harrald nurses' quarters and caused inevitable confusion there, too, particularly with the 'home sisters' (the title of the sister in charge of the nurses' quarters) who frequently challenged us. One in particular used to ask, 'Which one of the little beggars are you?'

In the staff cafeteria and elsewhere we were regularly greeted by people we didn't know who thought we were the other twin. We would just say hello back, as trying to explain took too long and we weren't always believed. One day we were both in the cafeteria together and a group of nurses sat down next to us with open mouths and shocked faces. In the group were people who knew one of us, but not both, and were not aware we were twins.

I recall a day when the cafeteria staff refused to give me lunch because they believed I'd already had mine. Guess who had been there before me?

Doctors would often approach one of us in the cafeteria, or elsewhere, and start commenting on or asking questions about a patient. We'd have to say, 'Sorry, wrong one.' After a while, when word got around that there were twin sister sisters, they would look at us with a questioning look and we'd say the name of our ward.

When we both wore the white uniform, stockings, shoes and bucket hat that registered nurses wore once the staff nurse year was finished, we made things even more difficult as we both dyed our hair (which we wore in exactly the same style) with

Magic Silver White, which turned fair hair to a white blonde colour. The director of nursing at the time walked behind us one day and loudly objected to the all-over white look, ordering us to make some change so it was easier for people to recognise which twin was which. I can't remember if we complied with the order . . . or not.

Twin trouble made our years at the RAH very memorable, and probably not just for us!

For three generations our family have walked these corridors as doctors, nurses and physiotherapists. Will miss feeling their presence in these old walls as I start a new walk down the road.

Royal Adelaide Hospital Registered Nurses' Association Inc.

Joan Durdin, AM

'To foster a spirit of friendship and mutual assistance among nurses.'

In the 'Rules Book' of the Royal Adelaide Hospital Registered Nurses' Association the above statement is the first item in a list of its objects. The Association was founded in1939. Though not widely known, even among nurses who have graduated from the hospital, it has played a significant part in many nurses' lives, while its influence has extended to the hospital itself and the wider community.

In the 1930s, society was recovering from the effects of an economic depression. Nurses' salaries, like all others, were low and there was still a degree of unemployment. Nursing leaders began to look at ways of improving the welfare of nurses and in response, in some hospitals, formed associations for graduate nurses. At the Adelaide Hospital, as it was then known, the matron took the initiative in 1938 to rally nurses to form the Adelaide Hospital Trained Nurses Association. It is now the Royal Adelaide Hospital Registered Nurses' Association Inc.

Members became enthusiastic fundraisers hoping to raise

money for the purchase of a holiday cottage for nurses, many of whom had no home of their own for recreation. This proved to be too ambitious, but the money raised formed the nucleus of a fund named in honour of an early, highly esteemed matron. In due course it became the Margaret Graham Benevolent Fund, reserved for the purpose of providing grants for individual nurses in financial difficulties.

In the meantime, they planned an annual program of events. Activities included social gatherings, bus trips, guest lectures, visits to institutions such as Lea Hurst (Home for Aged Nurses), games afternoons, and attendance at the Hospital's Foundation Day. The Association's funds supported various good causes, including a substantial contribution to the cost of a stained-glass window in the Hospital Chapel, the provision of electric typewriters to both the matron's office and the School of Nursing, facilities for display of uniforms in the School of Nursing, and a tree-planting project to modify the drab appearance of the hospital grounds after the last building program. Latterly the Association has made regular donations to provide books for nurses' postgraduate studies.

Over the years many members have given time, energy and enthusiasm to the work of the Association. However, while still a viable organisation, there has been concern for falling membership over the past twenty years.

One factor that influenced membership was the closure of the School of Nursing in 1993, when nursing education was transferred to the tertiary education sector. While recruitment from among newly graduated nurses was never strong, from that time onwards strength of the existing membership has grown, augmented by the support of those who joined on the basis of having spent at least one year as a registered nurse at the Hospital. Since 2015, two chapters have been formed, north and south of Adelaide.

An event in 2013 brought a challenge and an additional sense of purpose to the Association. It received a bequest from a former life member for the establishment of an annual scholarship to enable a country hospital nurse to undertake midwifery training. The Council accepted the challenge. A small group worked steadily over three years to enable this to happen. The first scholarship was awarded in March 2017.

As the time for closure of the 'old' Royal Adelaide Hospital approached, members of the Nurses' Association recognised the opportunity to extend the spirit of friendship and mutual assistance to their fellow nurses at the new RAH, and look forward to this development.

I walked in to the RAH speech pathology department nearly 25 years ago, and into the best years of my working life. What a wonderful team of people – so much of life shared together, so many enduring memories.

6 years within the ED Dept. Wonderful friendly staff. Third generation working at the RAH. Will be missed.

Have thoroughly enjoyed working as a radiographer since 1996. Will truly miss this place and sharing tearoom with ED, orderlies and volunteers.

I remember with fondness the wonderful staff in medical research over 25 years, in Medicine/ Gastroenterology and Rad Oncology. It was a ball.

March 1989. Started Acute Pain Service. Have seen over 59,600 patients since this time. Run by a dedicated APS team.

Turmeric Tales

Natasha Desai

I still remember the surprised look on the faces of my peers at the RAH Wellness Centre when I told them over afternoon tea that I had got a job at Yalata, a town in the Australian bush. Many were confused, most were concerned to make sure that I understood how remote it was, but overall there was unanimous support. I think it was that touch of adventure in people that made them want to know how I was going to do this, and wonder what stories I would return with. Little did I know that the experience would change my life.

I headed off to Yalata and my husband found work in Sydney. As new residents of Australia, we had no choice but to go where the work was.

I have a fear of four things: darkness, loneliness, Australian spiders and thunderstorms. They make me turn from my lioness-like exterior to a little kitten. My accommodation in Yalata had no streetlight and my gate overlooked the thick bush with its endless possibilities. (I will leave to everyone's imagination what I mean by possibilities.)

Amid dealing with just about everything you can think of in the health clinic at Yalata, I developed a boil. A boil in a rather private area of my body which made it impossible to see, and quite uncomfortable to walk and sit. With a general practitioner's visit only once a week, using medication from the pharmacy felt like a crime. While I squinted in discomfort, I thought to myself how I never before really appreciated living in the city with the best hospitals, healthcare, transport, restaurants, cafes and streetlights.

For two days the boil was the bane of my existence, and no drug on this planet (by which I mean the town in the middle of nowhere) was able to relieve it. Tired from the pain I finally caught some sleep, only to wake up next morning to a creepy crawly friend.

I stared at the spider on the ceiling of my house, numb from the thought of having to act to deal with it. After twenty minutes of locking my gaze on him, I decided to shower and leave for work. I have no clue why I thought that doing nothing was my best option! I described my encounter to every possible employee, who by then had lost all respect for me as their manager with my continuous blabber about a spider.

'It's probably a huntsman,' one of my colleagues said, in complete disbelief of my agony. 'Just whack it with your shoe,' said another, giggling at me.

The boil, the spider, the anxiety and my all-glorious realisation of going home to no one, culminated to test my sanity. When I returned to my house, the spider was exactly where I left him. Cursing, but appreciating my luck, I ran to fetch a broom. I whacked the spider hard with the back of the broom, only to miss it several times. I can assure you that I yelled louder with every miss. I must have confused the spider so much that he did not move, despite my complete lack of confidence and skill. Finally, he fell on the floor. If anyone had said to me at that instant that killing a spider is bad luck, they would have suffered the same fate as the spider.

I had little time to celebrate since my boil had become even more painful. I didn't know what to do, believing that one-centimetre boil would be the end of me. I made the tastiest dal that evening, and ate it as though it was my last. Reflecting on my adventurous day I remembered that I was an Indian and that I should possess the ability to find *moksha* in every breath I take. I also remembered that I use turmeric every day and that I was a big idiot. I made a paste using drinking water and applied it to the boil in the extraordinary confidence that I had found the solution. I know I brought the fate of living in this lonely area upon myself, but it was the Indian in me that rose to the occasion.

Next morning the boil was gone, but the skies challenged the land that day with a thunderstorm that banged open my main gate. I called my husband on his cellphone and walked out in the dark and closed my gate. I still don't know how I found the courage to do that. It must have been love. Love from my husband who I hadn't seen in months and missed every day. Every time I see couples quarrelling on baseless issues, I have the urge to tell them how lucky they are to have each other day after day.

I worked for several weeks and then had a week off. I couldn't wait to tell my RAH friends about my experiences over those first few weeks. I told everyone who would listen about my adventures.

I love both the RAH and Yalata now and I'm learning to appreciate the small things. Small things like the joy of teatime with friends, so that I can share my turmeric tales.

Migrating from India on a student visa in 2008. Student nurse here 2008. Hospital sponsored my visa and employed me in 2009. Thanks RAH.

RAH Volunteer Service – Lavender Lads and Ladies

Extract of Annual Dedication Service, Inter-denominational and Inter-faith RAH Chaplaincy

CHAPLAIN

Today we have given thanks and honour the service given by Lavender Lads and Ladies. Let us renew our commitment for the next twelve months.

RESPONSE

We, as members of Lavender Lads and Ladies volunteer service, commit ourselves to be an integral part of the Royal Adelaide Hospital for the next twelve months.

We commit ourselves to our faith and understanding and from that draw strength and guidance as we help provide an atmosphere conducive to recovery, offering words of cheer and encouragement.

May we respect the privacy and feelings of patients, relatives, friends and other members of our team and co-operate at all times with the community of the Royal Adelaide Hospital.

As part of this team, we will be reliable in our tasks and relationships, showing compassion and patience, without seeking personal gain or praise to the best of our ability

CHAPLAIN

Go as people proud of our heritage into an unknown future full of great possibilities. Be a people full of compassion and kindness. Strengthen the fainthearted, support the weak, help the afflicted and honour everyone. Go in peace and may the God of peace walk with you.

ALL

Amen

As an interpreter (Spanish) it was wonderful to meet so many wonderful people: patients and staff. The information we facilitate is not always nice or easy, but it was always handled professionally and compassionately by the medical staff.

I have worked at the RAH as an anaesthetic agency nurse over a 12-year period. I have loved the experience from the dynamic team to the complex case mix. Thank you.

Working as an OT at the RAH has meant sharing lots of fabulous lunches in our department. It was always a friendly space with lots of noise at lunchtime.

In the short time I have been here, I have met not only great co-workers but great friends. Thank you to the amazing team in the eye department.

I have been a volunteer with the heritage unit for 5 years. It was a wonderful moment when I first saw 'Corporal Coles' hand'; Dr Florey's original penicillin growth. So many treasures we have.

Since I was a medical student I have always aspired to work at the RAH. I am really delighted that I have finally got a chance and so great that I will now be working at the new RAH – the Centre of Excellence!

Places, Spaces, a Ghost – and Goodbye

Tuesday, 5 September 2017

Anne, a physiotherapist, and Harry, a nurse, loved to take their breaks outside in the tree-filled surrounds of the RAH. The kiosk in the main reception area led out onto an area in front of the hospital, on North Terrace, where patients and staff gathered to eat, talk with their visitors, or just sit and relax. The two friends loved to have lunch there on a fine day.

On their last full day at the old RAH, Anne and Harry made a point of sitting in their favourite spot for a few minutes in their lunch break, before getting up to look at the buildings for the last time.

'Funny how a group of buildings can get to you,' Harry said. 'I want to do one last round of them all.'

They walked across to the East Wing and then back along the walkway that led to the Emergency Department. It had closed that morning and it was strange to see it empty, lacking the ambulances usually parked outside.

'The ambulances will be busy ferrying patients to the new hospital,' Anne said. 'Just think, we'll be there tomorrow too.'

They walked back to the front entrance, past the Allied Health building, then past the Margaret Graham and Eleanor Harrald buildings, and down towards the residential wing and the chapel, one of their favourite places with its beautiful stained glass.

On the way, Harry thought about the experiences he'd had in some of the wards and departments of the hospital. Night duty, with its very different atmosphere, was a particularly vivid memory. It was usually much quieter than in the daytime and walking around with a torch changed the way everything looked. There had been times when he had not been able to look over his shoulder, convinced someone – or something – was following him.

The East Wing, said to be haunted by the Grey Nurse, was particularly spooky. Many people reported they had heard or seen her and of course people used the stories to scare their colleagues. Harry would never admit it, but remembered being nervous on many occasions as he came to a corner, or walked down a corridor on his own. 'I wonder if the Grey Nurse will transfer,' he said, with a grin.

'I wouldn't put it past her,' Anne said. 'Every hospital needs a resident ghost.'

Cardiac arrest in A4, and someone went 'round and reassured the patients. Who? The Grey Nurse.

I remember the Grey Nurse . . . I pretended to be her and scared nurses coming out of theatre.

5 to 6 am in the stairwell in East Wing and there was the clinking of chains. Must have been the Grey Nurse!

Lovely as a Tree

Joan Durdin, AM

Nurses at the Adelaide Hospital had good reason to appreciate its tree-clad grounds. In the early years of the nineteenth century two institutions that were part of the hospital, the Isolation Hospital and the Consumptives Home, were separated from the main hospital building. Nurses interviewed years later told tales of their fearfulness of the sounds of the night – the possums, the creaking of the branches of trees and the human noises of sleeping patients as they moved among them in the semi darkness.

By day, there was a greater appreciation of the trees, which were a significant part of the environment. Those who were on duty in the wards of the main hospital learnt to navigate the trees and shrubs forming part of the boundary between the hospital and the Botanic Gardens, and stories are told of nurses creeping through the barrier into the Gardens at Christmas time, to obtain greenery for decorating their wards.

When off-duty, student nurses also took advantage of the Gardens. In twos and threes, they chose to wander down, books under their arms, to settle on the lawns where to all intents and purposes they studied for exams. Without question they also gained some valued recreation. At other times they gained the permission of ward sisters to take patients in wheelchairs for a thirty-minute walk along the well-kept paths of the Gardens on a sunny afternoon.

In the 1930s and 1940s, nurses who were confined to bed on the veranda of the sick bay, adjacent to Light Ward, had a wide view to the east. Canvas blinds protected them from the elements at night, but in the morning the horizon was a sea of treetops. Some nurses claim to have counted the trees, as a diversion.

Over the years tree removal within the grounds of the hospital was inevitable, to allow space for new buildings as the hospital grew. One tree-loving charge nurse is credited with the prevention of removal of a lovely plane tree adjacent to Frome Ward. After a succession of requests, she won her case and the tree was spared. At the time of the transfer of the last patient to the new hospital, it still stood, near the entrance to the Residential Wing, with a plaque under it testifying to her persistence.

For the next 'tree' story we are indebted to the hospital's works manager of the 1960s. He instructed the removal of, among other plants, two magnificent Moreton Bay fig trees in the front garden of what was then known as Austral House. He ascertained that another government institution, a little way down Frome Road, had need of large leaves for its precious elephant. The informal transaction included the agreement that the Zoo would provide workmen to cut down the leaves and branches, as required, and transfer them, while the Hospital was saved the cost of this work and could prepare for filling the vacant space in the lawn. Such a story might also be entitled 'Good Neighbours'.

SMOKE-FREE

The Lady in the Lift

Barbara Smith

I have been a Lavender Lady at the RAH for about twenty-two years and, as you can imagine, I have spent a lot of time waiting for and using the lifts. There have been many times when I've heard those all so familiar words (echoing my thoughts): 'Why is this lift taking so long?' Or, 'I wish it would hurry up.' Or, 'I think I will take the stairs.'

After many years, a decision was made to renovate the lifts. The new lifts had shiny polished walls and bright new lit-up buttons. Maybe it was thought this would somehow make the lift go faster but, alas, this was not the case. However, there was now a recorded voice in the new lifts. I called her the 'Lady in the Lift', and liked to imagine her as real.

I was in the lift with an orderly once and, as there were only the two of us in there at the time, I talked about the Lady in the Lift. The orderly looked at me, confused, and I continued. 'I wonder if the Lady ever gets tired of saying: *Level 1, Level 7 . . .*'

The orderly smiled and continued the theme. 'She would have to be skinny to fit in between the walls.'

'Well, that's true,' I said. 'And her arms would get tired, pulling cables up and down all day.'

What sort of stories would the Lady in the Lift hear and, if there were a little window for her to peek through, how many interesting people would she see? What would the Lady in the Lift think of the man with a guide dog who knows exactly which level to get out at? Does she know how helpful she's been when her lovely voice says 'Level 6' just as the door opens, so he can step out knowing he is on the right floor?

One Lavender Lad told me about how he dropped his phone in the lift and the back fell off and slid, with the battery, through the gap where the doors slide along the floor. He wondered whether he could retrieve it from the bottom of the lift well once the old hospital was demolished (clearly I'm not the only one with a dry sense of humour). That got me thinking how many other objects must have fallen down to the bottom of the shaft. If the Lady in the Lift collected all the coins that have probably fallen through the gap, she could have been rich by now.

I have had my photo taken in the outpatients lift with another Lavender Lady. It was when the Lavender Lads and Ladies were escorts for patients who weren't sure which lift level to exit at for their clinic. We had a little stool to sit on and a laminated list of all the clinics on every level. People were so grateful, and it wasn't bad if you liked a sit-down job and didn't mind riding up and down in the lift all day.

All sorts of people, and even dogs, have gone in and out of the lifts of the RAH. I'm sure many strange and amusing things have happened there, so next time you get into one and you think of how much time you have spent waiting, or are annoyed about the one and only lift that has just broken down, think about the recorded voice and imagine the Lady in the Lift.

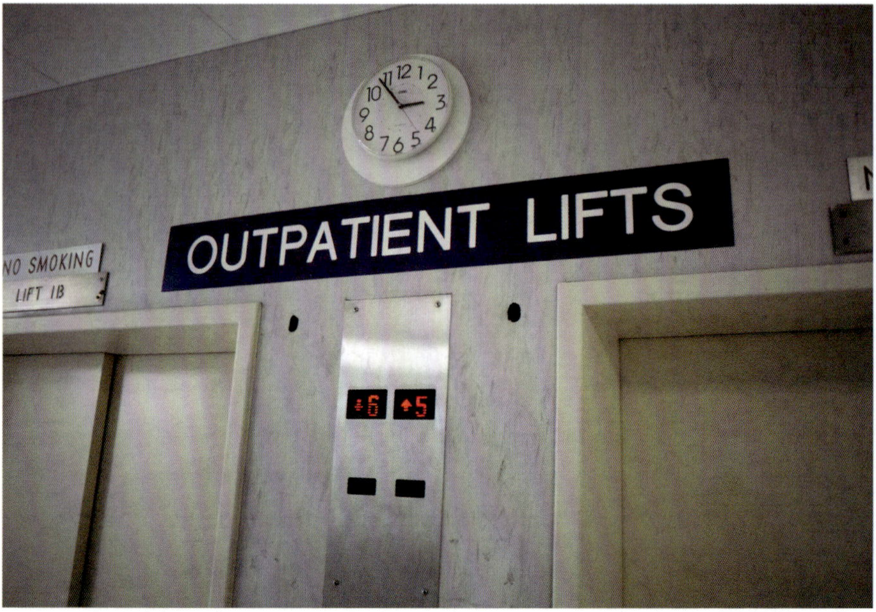
OUTPATIENT LIFTS
NO SMOKING
LIFT IB

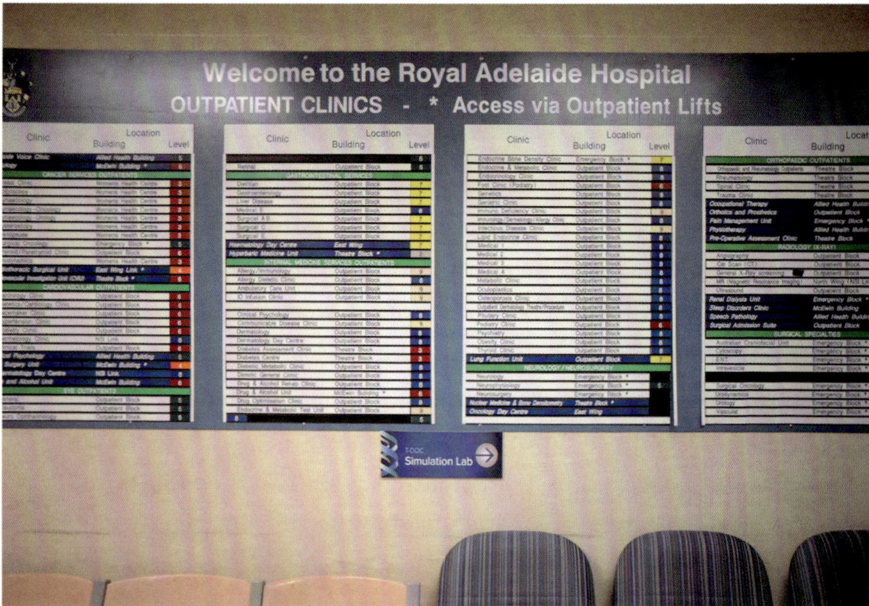

Welcome to the Royal Adelaide Hospital
OUTPATIENT CLINICS - * Access via Outpatient Lifts
Clinic
Location
Building
Level
Simulation Lab

RAH Botanic Walk Murals

Kaye Challinger

During the early 1990s, research undertaken in the United States suggested that it was not only the healthcare received that affected the wellbeing and recovery of patients. A body of evidence collected within the health/architectural world shows that patients' recovery improved within environments that provided those elements of life that we all take for granted – namely good design, music, art, light and colour.

As the Royal Adelaide Hospital was a public hospital, a view was held by both staff and the general community that it would always be there and could be relied upon in time of need; that it was a fundamental part of the Adelaide community. To foster this, a strategy was conceived to combine the development of the design research and the desire to have the Hospital open to its public. The health promotion area was encouraged to develop a program. This included utilising the talent and willingness of the nearby Music Conservatorium, encouraging students to bring their instruments to areas and wards within the hospital, to provide music for the patients.

Another major component of the program was the provision of artwork within the hospital. An artist associated with the Botanic Gardens provided ten large inked outlines of scenes within the Botanic Gardens. The canvasses were on tables in the main entrance foyer for some months and staff and visitors were invited to paint in an area of choice. The progress of the paintings over the months generated considerable interest within the hospital; nurses were seen doing a part of a canvass during their lunchtime break.

A selection of the final paintings was hung as wall murals on the newly created Level 5 street within the hospital. The gallery also provided space for beginning artists to display their works for sale. A staff member from the kitchen was one of those who responded and his particular story was featured in an edition of *SA Life*.

Photographs of musicians playing in the wards were also displayed in the gallery, which bounds the services and teaching block, and also has links to the theatres, the North and East wings, and the most recently created P-Wing.

A picture is worth a thousand words . . . a building is worth a lifetime of memories.

SECURITY
SURVEILLANCE CAMERAS & ALARMS IN USE
REPORT THEFT
Peters
Peters
Dive in
peters.com.au

R.A.H. RESEARCH FUND
NEWSAGENCY
Shoebox
HER
HER

I'm going to miss the kiosk meatballs more than anything.

Angela put ice cream in the vac chute and sent it and broke the machine.

In the ward in the 1970s the kitchen staff would hand out drinks from a trolley for morning and afternoon tea. In winter, the trolley had large stainless-steel jugs full of thick hot vegetable soup, which was very popular with nurses and interns. I always associate the East Wing with the smell of vegetable soup.

The small room in the nurses' station, 'a little chill chat' place in burns unit will be missed.

Goodbye to the Eleanor Harrald building where many students have passed through the doors to take on courses and qualifications that have enhanced their working careers in SA. Now heading towards their new careers at the nRAH.

It is here that I've found myself again. Thank you, RAH!

TAKE CARE
ON STAIRS

HONOUR ROLL

Untold Tales

Soumyadeep Bhattacherya

Her dreamy eyes are numb,
reflecting the mystery hidden.

A thousand dazzling galaxies that
take leap into sweetest fairytale.

Smile can snatch the sunshine,
to make flowers dance in rain.

The feel of feathery hair,
slips from mind now and then.

Eyes could narrate untold stories
of a hundred unfinished chapters.

Working at RAH for over 40 years.
I had a working life of fun, fulfilment
and a feeling I had made a difference!
I was supported and given
opportunities and lucky to be involved
in some SA firsts.

40 years of happy, sad,
funny, inspiring, learning,
teaching and, above all,
caring memories.

21 years!
Think I may cry.
Going to miss you ward Q8.

Fondest memories of a wonderful 13
year career at this beautiful RAH.
Forever grateful for the greatest
experience and knowledge gained
during my time here.
Bye RAH!

Farewell Old Friend

Claire Colbey

For more than a hundred and sixty years,
the old RAH existed.
Countless patients, young and old,
the medical staff assisted.
The nurses in their uniforms,
their hair in a tidy bun,
long black frocks, then neat red capes,
from starched white caps to none.

The patients, the visitors,
the staff and volunteers,
each hold their memories
collected through the years.
From happy stories, funny stories,
tales that led us to cheers,
to sad stories, poignant stories,
tales that brought us to tears.

But it's not just the folk who made this place,
(though they surely played their part),

this old building had a presence,
a dignity, a heart.
It had a culture all its own,
which now, it seems, is 'dated',
but things that stand the test of time
should not be under-rated.

Can bricks and mortar,
and old lino' floors,
and leaking roofs,
and creaking doors,
and empty stairwells,
and dungeons dim,
cause melancholy
from within?

May the ghosts of the past
protect you . . .
you are the resting place.

The answer is – 'Yes, of course this is true',
this stately old place became a part of you,
as year upon year
it wrapped its walls
around all who sheltered
within its halls.
So, raise a glass and say out loud,
'Farewell, old friend, you did us proud.'

I have met many professionals here! A place where my nursing career started. Too many memories. This place will be dearly missed.

Dear RAH,
I'll miss you! This hospital is my first job out of nursing school. So memorable! Feels like home. See you at the other side of the town.
Cheers.

Thanks for your great care of my father and mother.

Wow, wow & wow.
From a grand old lady to a young woman.

A wonderful place to remember because of the many caring people who work there.

North Tce
Robson Theatre
North Wing

From the Old to the New

15 July 1840

The foundation stone was laid for a new Adelaide Hospital, near Hackney Road.

January 1841

The new Adelaide Hospital received its first patients.

1856

The hospital moved to the current site of the old Royal Adelaide Hospital.

1939

The Royal prefix was granted.

Wednesday, 6 September 2017

The old RAH, mostly empty of patients now, buzzed with expectation. The last patients would be transferred to the new hospital this morning. The media started turning up early, and several VIPs too. This would be a great occasion, albeit an emotional one.

The last patient was transferred well ahead of time, and with a televised farewell. After that, staff continued to transfer anything that still needed to be moved, until finally the transition to the new RAH was complete.

At the new RAH, staff and patients began to get to know their new home, while at the old RAH, security checked the building and began the task of locking it up and installing fences around its perimeter. The old RAH site will eventually have a multitude of uses, and some of the heritage buildings will be retained. One amazing era had finished and a new one had begun.

But wait, was that a nurse in grey at the window? There! In that East Wing window.

All the Goodbye Notes

20 years of service, many special times here! Will miss it.

Great place to work in 1970 and in 2017. I will miss the traditions and heritage.

Thank you old RAH for wonderful memories of my 27 years' service at DSS.

Just two and a half years shy. Love you!

Thank you for a warm welcome from moving to RAH from TQEH. Can't wait for the next chapter at the nRAH.

Made my 30 years, started August 1987 until August 2017. Lots of fun memories. Goodbye East Wing.

GNP year 2003.

A wonderful start to my career. Been here 11 years now!

Wonderful memories from working in ward R8 and the chest clinic. Being trained by the amazing nurses and other staff has been great, and meeting some amazing friends. Wonderful memories.

21 years! Think I may cry. Going to miss you ward Q8.

Fondest memories of a wonderful 13 year career at this beautiful RAH. Forever grateful for the greatest experience and knowledge gained during my time here. Bye RAH!

30 years of great memories. Bye old RAH!

40 years of happy, sad, funny, inspiring, learning, teaching and, above all, caring memories.

The old RAH has been my second home in the last 2 decades. Too many good and some not so good memories. Met friends. I will surely miss it.

I have laughed many times over the last 28 years. It's been an education in life.

24 August 1984 was my first day. I was 17. I'm still here!

It was wonderful to experience and enjoy working at this old RAH for the last 14 years. I am thankful to be part of this hospital, it has taught me so much. I've met so many lovely people working here. (Q8)

Maggots and MET calls. Morphine and mayhem. Laughter, friendship, family. 15 years of excellence and commitment. Mending wounds and hearts. Helping people to live and die with dignity.

Have spent 32 years in this wonderful hospital. Lots of great memories.

20 years of memories. Now on a new adventure.

14 years of fond memories.

For 37 years we have been family. I will miss you all!

A great place to start my career – lots of support. Now 12 years later I am able to support others.

28 years of fond memories. Bye RAH.

So many beautiful memories, lots of laughs with colleagues and patients. Loved working 10 years in this place and looking forward to working many more years at the new RAH.

Been part of this lovely organisation since 29 June 2009. Love RAH and I'm proud to be part of it. Changed my career, miles ahead! Loving RAH, loving SA.

34 years at RAH. Good memories. I know the old and the new. Goodbye old RAH!

Leaving the hospital after 14 years, I came back in 2006 and have worked a total of 25 years here. I'm proud to be an enrolled nurse and highly skilled in my job and will look back on so many memories here.

I joined the old RAH in February 2010. Since then I am working as an RN here.

It was very nice working here. Very sweet old memories.

I have worked here 37 years and the RAH is like a second home and the staff I work with are like my family.

Only here for a year. Loving the people, staff and, of course, the coffee.

Friends made at the RAH have become lifelong friends for 40 years.

10 years of fun, friendship and treating some very inspirational patients.

Farewell old RAH, have enjoyed my 23 years of service!

Made great friends. 1958–1961.

29 years of fond memories. Thank you RAH!

14 years in RAH have been the best 14 years out of my 42 years of nursing. Love this place!

Great friendships over 25 years. Have become a work family.

The ASU opened 2012. Been at North Terrace for 10 years.

28 years of memories.

From General Recovery to Endoscopy to IBD nursing. Bye RAH!

26 years of service, first ward A8 with Dr B. Stairway to heaven and the tales of the grey nurse. Sneaking into the stairwell to have a cigarette with the night CNC walking up saying 'put these out before I get there'.
Will always have the fondest of memories.

Being here since 1979, I have a lifetime of memories.
I simply love the way the RAH cares for everyone and anyone.

'Rock on' group 862. 31 years and still going!

RAH brought me from the UK 9 years before as a Cardiac Cath Lab Nurse.
My awesome 9 years. I will really miss my first workplace in Australia.

Working at RAH for over 40 years. I had a working life of fun, fulfilment and a feeling I had made a difference! I was supported and given opportunities and lucky to be involved in some SA firsts.

My time at the RAH has been short and sweet since 2015. It's been awesome working in the oldest hospital but will be amazing to work in the new RAH.

Over 30 years, have worked with a multitude of wonderful staff.
End of an era, here's to a new beginning.

36 years of fond memories. Sad to say goodbye really. #Newchapter!

Memories of A4, A6 and A7, C8 and P6. The last 10 years of fun and laughs.

I worked in the RAH stores from 2001–2005. I had a very enjoyable time here. Will be sorry to see it go, but life goes on.

I can't believe it has been 30 years! So many good memories and bad too! Being chased down the passage by a patient swinging a drip stand, meeting patients who have been cured and came back to the ward with chocolates*.
*Chocolates given to nurses from patients do not make you fat!

Started at the RAH in April 1981. I have seen many changes over the years; this is the biggest change of them all.

12 years spent with wonderful caring colleagues.Good times and bad, always a friendly face and kind, caring shoulder to lean on.
Here's to making new memories.

After more than 20 years, I will miss it!

I started here on 1 June 1986. I made it to the 31st anniversary. Bit sad at leaving.

34 years I have walked these corridors, they are like old friends.

20 years, oh so long. Weekend lunches. I won't miss the old place!
Q8

Will miss the old RAH. I have worked for 9 years with a good team, but very excited to work in the new RAH. All the best, new Royal Adelaide Hospital.

It's been an awesome 17 years here. So many memories. Will definitely be missed.

Enjoyed my time here over the last 10 years.

I remember thinking I would never find my way around this hospital all those years ago. Now I have to learn to navigate around the new RAH.

35 years of amazing memories and many, many changes.
The end of an era, very sad to say goodbye.

40 years and loved every minute of a great place to work.

17 years of fond memories. Goodbye RAH!

10 years of wonderful friends and patients, sad to see the change.

Fond memories, trained in 1977 and have witnessed many changes!

Been here 24 years. Too many memories to write.
Lots of amazing times with amazing people.

Spent the best years of my youth here!

I am going to miss my 10 years of second home. I will cherish all the memories.

Thankyou RAH, 37 years of fun and laughter!

After arrival in Australia, nice to work for a wonderful place with a great team!

I walked in to the RAH speech pathology department nearly 25 years ago, and into the best years of my working life. What a wonderful team of people – so much of life shared together, so many enduring memories.

Got my dream job at the cardiac theatres old RAH.

ICU, so supportive to new staff. My favourite place to work.

Have thoroughly enjoyed working as a radiographer since 1996. Will truly miss this place and sharing tearoom with ED, orderlies and volunteers.

The fun, laughter and teamwork of being with my orthopaedic nurse colleagues. My first orthopaedic ward round on R3 was on a Wednesday morning with a neat ward and patients sitting out of bed! Vasovagal or not. 23 years.

6 years within the ED Dept. Wonderful friendly staff.
Third generation working at the RAH.

Will be missed.

Sitting on IMDB getting paid a mint on public holidays.

2006 – new ICU opened.

Night duty in neurosurgery in mid 1990s. I didn't need glasses to see my fob watch.

My best memory of the RAH was meeting an amazing group of exceptional nurses on ward C6 who will always be good friends.

Saw my first and only triple traumatic amputation in my first week in ED in 2015.

ASU, such a great team to work with! Excited for a new and improved building!

Made many good friends records medical admin, 2013–2017.

My first day at the RAH was as a third year physiotherapy student. I was so impressed by ICU and all the staff here . . . I knew straight away it was exactly where I wanted to work.

I have worked at the RAH as an anaesthetic agency nurse over a 12 year period. I have loved the experience from the dynamic team to the complex case mix. Thank you.

In the short time I have been here, I have met not only great co-workers but great friends. Thank you to the amazing team in the eye department.

Afterhours CSCs, what a crazy, fabbie job! Loved every minute! Good work!

Working as an outpatients admin has been a great experience and being in a diverse group of hardworking individuals has been a rewarding journey.

As an interpreter (Spanish) it was wonderful to meet so many wonderful people: patients and staff. The information we facilitate is not always nice or easy, but it was always handled professionally and compassionately by the medical staff.

Great opportunities opened up to me when I first started in vascular then in the internal medical department.

Thank you to the beautiful staff on ward Q5 for all the help and support to me as a student nurse. I will miss you all!

Many good times on the old C8/D8 when I started nursing. Farewell old RAH. On to the new RAH and new good times.

I was in the first group of GNPs Jan '99 to wear the polo tops. We got many looks and remarks saying 'You look like one of the maintenance workers'.

Best hospital bed corners award goes to Rick of ward R5 followed by Ron, also of R5.

R5 hands down the best ward, full of amazing staff. New RAH here we come.

Working in the old ESS. Many happy memories.

The views from the C6 Cancer Centre over the botanic gardens and hills. A great escape for patients.

All the fun, crazy, hilarious moments, joyful, sad times looking after those in C3. Thank you.

Many memories over the past 30 years from the RAH and SA Pathology (IMVS). Some sad, with loss of family lovingly cared for by the nurses, and many happier ones. One door closes and another opens – here's to new beginnings at the new RAH and new memories.

March 1989. Started acute pain service. Have seen over 59,600 patients since this time. Run by a dedicated APS team.

Since 1996 when I joined the Biomedical Engineering staff, I have seen great advances in equipment used for patient care. The 21st century really has arrived in the Royal Adelaide Hospital.

I was welcomed with open arms to Q5 and I've had the best year of my life working with a team of dedicated professionals. Thank you RAH.

My first full time job! RN in RAH ICU. Thank you for the opportunity!

Q7 GIU. Best team of nurses and Drs to work with.

Working as an OT at the RAH has meant sharing lots of fabulous lunches in our department. It was always a friendly space with lots of noise at lunchtime.

It's the RAH way or the highway! Awesome intensive care memories with a fab team.

I have worked at SA Pathology at the RAH site for 9 years. I've had a wonderful time working with fantastic people. I also share wonderful memories with my father while he was cared for at RAH.

Farewell from SA Pathology. I'm pretty sure the old building is haunted.
Ha Ha! No more night shift! Thank you!

So proud to be part of an amazing speech pathology department for over 25 years. What a team!

Home for nearly 20 years. Fond memories of B4.

Thank you ICU RAH.

I remember with fondness the wonderful staff in medical research over 25 years, in Medicine/Gastroenterology and Rad Oncology. It was a ball.

Nights in ESS managing major trauma cases in P1 and P2.

Ditto, I second that.

Ditto!

ASMU 2014–2017. Best time ever.

My best memories are of my training days during late 50s and early 60s and my time volunteering in the Kiosk.

Training at the RAH back in the 80s and living in the residential wing with all the girls on level 5 . . . best 3 years of my nursing career. Being part of the retrieval service MEDIFLIGHT for 12 years was physically demanding but so rewarding.

Being a student with RAH in 2009, a week after completing my EN diploma I was an employee on the ward where I finished my placement, and am still there today.

Goodbye to the Eleanor Harrald building. Many students have passed through the doors to take on courses and qualifications that have enhanced their working careers in SA. Heading towards new directions at the nRAH.

I have met many professionals here! A place where my nursing career started. Too many memories. This place will be dearly missed.

I will never forget my first job as an RN at the RAH. To be part of the move in my TPPP year is one I will never forget.

The RAH is where I began my journey as a nurse. I have met many amazing people here both staff and patients. I have experienced some very heart-felt stories. I am sad to leave the old RAH but excited for the journey to the new RAH.

My training group was group 771 (1977) and we have just celebrated our 40th anniversary. It was a wonderful few years of training! Sad to say goodbye to the RAH.

Thank you RAH for allowing me to commence my nursing career on ward S5.

I trained and lived here back 30 odd years ago. So much history for me here! Sad to say goodbye. My mother and half my family trained here.

Old fashioned training in the 80s.

Trained in 1980 in the last group of enrolled nurses trained at the RAH. End of an era!

Thanks so much for giving me an opportunity to learn and start my career here. I love this place and will be always grateful.

I recall ward rounds as a med student in Light and Flinders. Moved into the new north wing as an intern in 1970. That to me was the new RAH!

Working at the hospital as a student has helped me to grow into a better health professional, and built me up for my career. Goodbye RAH!

Student nurse training, friendships – teamwork – night duty.

This hospital RAH shaped me as a nurse. I will always have fond memories of learning and working here.

From past memories of a dental nurse training under the RAH banner in 1970s–1990s to a receptionist working in outpatients years later. Wonderful memories – 2 lifetimes of career paths.

Since I was a medical student I have always aspired to work at the RAH. I am really delighted that I have finally got a chance and so great that I will now be working at the new RAH – the Centre of Excellence!

Starting my career here has been a great experience.

I started my nursing career at the RAH! Had some amazing experiences and met some amazing people.

June 2008, when I started at the Royal Adelaide Hospital as one of the lucky 'GNPs'. RAH has been part of my everyday place to go. Every day is different, brought tears to some, happiness and hope to many.

I recall as a young enthusiastic trainee enrolled nurse at age 26 learning how to do a 'cradle lift' with my senior nurse and getting a little more than expected! To the delight of an elderly fragile lady patient! Welcome to nursing at the RAH.

I started on 1/10/79 as a Trainee Enrolled Nurse. A couple of years doing a 6 month Orthopaedic Emergency Nursing Certificate. Working in theatre I have scrubbed for operations but also my experience has seen me work as the plaster room nurse, a hyperbaric nurse and much more. I've also done an anaesthetic certificate.

First shift I got locked in the stairwell banging on the door until someone came to my rescue. Very embarrassed!

Learnt how to be a doctor here. I remember the surgeon holding a lady as she cried just before her leg was amputated.

Started working at the RAH in 2013. I love working at the RAH, thanks for the memories. I will miss this old building.

Thank you for the education, opportunities and laughs. Countless trips around the hospital with my patients.

It has been a great opportunity to develop my skills and knowledge!

Ringing other students overnight pretending we were ED with a new patient.

Arrived from Tassie for a new adventure and joined our speciality team. Dealt with ups and downs of life. The RAH was a good home and the new RAH will be our new home in a few days.

The Royal Adelaide Hospital will always hold a special place in my heart! My first year of nursing as a TPPP. All the staff are amazing and I am super grateful I got to spend 9 months here and be a part of the move.

Will miss you, where my nursing career started.

Student nurse in the 80s encapsulated immersive learning. Teaching nurse staff today remains an enormous privilege.

Migrating from India on a student visa in 2008. Student nurse here 2008. Hospital sponsored my VISA and employed me in 2009. Thanks RAH.

Dear RAH, I'll miss you! This hospital is my first job out of nursing school – so memorable! Feels like home. See you at the other side of the town.

I trained in old RAH as an enrolled nurse, moving on to RN . . . It has been a bumpy ride but full of wonderful experiences, which made me a good nurse. Goodbye old RAH, thank you for the wonderful time.

I remember 14/11/77, my first day at the RAH, when I was taken, as a lowly base-grade physiotherapist, to be personally welcomed by the hospital administrator. Times have certainly changed.

Learning on the wards as a medical student.

The feeling of terror on my very first day compared to my absolute confidence I have today, thanks to all my wonderful colleagues at the RAH.

I trained here from 1983–1986. I will always remember sister H clip clopping down the corridor with her white dress, cap and red cape on night shift. We were terrified of her but respected her so much!

The RAH has been where I completed my internship and my medical training. I have made so many friends during my time here.

After 22 years at the kiosk, happy memories of all my friends and staff, love you all.

Nina's smiling face and hot coffee every morning.

I'm going to miss the kiosk meatballs more than anything.

I'll miss the sweet potato chips from the kiosk!

I will miss some of the beautiful trees around the hospital. Spring will be tomorrow and the trees are budding. I will miss their shade and freshness.

I will miss sitting on the balcony of Revive on 5 looking over the botanical gardens whilst drinking my morning coffee

Mornings watching the sunrise in the RMO society lounge after a long and gruelling shift as the medical night's intern.

I was the last nurse to be interviewed in 1978 for intake in '79. It was a long wait, with hundreds before me. Nan C interviewed me then drove me home (I knew I was in). I was in 791 and it was quite an eye opener for a 19 yr old. There were many things I hadn't been exposed to . . . after a year I had seen heaps. I loved working in A6 and wanted to stay there. Unfortunately this was not to be. I asked to be in a busy area. I ended up in ED with sister Sam. I learnt so much there and stayed for about 15 years. I was the first punk nurse to work in ED with crazy hair, but that was ok off the collar. Now all convention changed and anything goes yay! P.S. Still love punk.

It all started in 1999 as new uni graduate RN on the GNP program. 12 years of ICU with permanent nights 7 on and 7 off, and I still question how I did it.

I am in Anaesthetics theatre, I see it all, and now a move to the new place.

I did my graduate nurse program here in 1999, then didn't want to work anywhere else. Many happy memories.

My nursing journey began here at the RAH.

Early years as a medical student learning the ropes.

Student nurses in 811, after the Eleanor Harrald building, learned that families sitting next to them in McDonalds will leave their meals rather than listen to conversations about nursing 'highlights'!

Dear RAH,
Wonderful introduction, have learned so much! Love looking after my patients.

Yes, it's a funny old collection of buildings, but it's the people who care enough to make patients happy, expediting good outcomes. We don't need to lose this in the move!

Wow, wow & wow. From a grand old lady to a young woman.

Held hands,
Dried tears,
Laughed, cried,
Saved lives and watched last breaths.

Many years full of tears, tantrums, much laughter and learning.
Will miss the old place.

Great place to work, will be missed.

Goodbye and good luck.

Won't be missing all the maintenance.

RAH. Wonderful place to work.

I was here.

It is here that I've found myself again. Thank you RAH!

Will miss the familiar corridors, the places to think in the chaos.
New place and new memories ahead.

End of an era. Goodbye ol' RAH.

Thanks RAH, it's been a big help staying with you. You will never be forgotten.

The lifelong friendships during my working life at the RAH are the most valuable memory from the RAH.

Lots of fun times and laughter. Santa and Easter are the best. Will be missed, however memories are forever.

Fantastic service to the sick. Have worked here for 4 weeks and everyone is wonderful.

So many wonderful memories I have here. Love my work, sometimes bad days and good days. I will miss you all.

Dear RAH, we will miss you, thank you for the great time.

So many wonderful memories. Moving into Eleanor Harrald on the 1st day of staffing.

You will be missed.

So long, farewell, you'll be missed.

Met my lifelong friends thanks to the RAH.

Goodbye Old RAH. Such a wonderful history. It's on to bigger and better things at the new location.

Treasured memories.

I'm going to miss you, old girl.

So long and thanks for all the muffins.

End of an era! It's been a journey to remember. Farewell old RAH.

Thanks for all my friends at the RAH.

Bye RAH, we love you but it's time to find a new love.

It's a wonderful experience working at RAH, got to meet beautiful people and shared great memories. I will surely miss the people, place.

It's been an amazing journey here at the RAH. Excited yet sad with the moving but it is in a good way. Going to miss everything here including the people and the place.

All the beautiful friends that have become family, lots of catch up lunches at the new RAH to come.

Was a great place to work, and will be a great place to work.

Friendships among all the different depts working together, teamwork at its best.

Thanks for a good experience in RAH. Looking forward to the new RAH.

Good memories! Great RAH! New beginning at the nRAH!

Good colleagues, good co-workers, happy patients, good times. Goodbye old RAH.

Had great fun working here in the old RAH. And new RAH all the best!

Thank you for the memories.

I have met so many wonderful people while working here. It's going to be strange not coming to work here anymore.

Good memories, great RAH. New beginnings at the nRAH.

I'm going to miss my old friends and the party here at the locker rooms at tea break.

A wonderful institution, sad to see the old RAH retire.

Old RAH, will miss you. Here is where my dear brother passed away in the care of caring nurses.

Many good memories, so many new ones to make at the nRAH.

Can't wait to work in one of the best technological hospitals in the world. P.S. RAH is the first ever place to offer me a permanent job.

We will miss you. Good memories.

A wonderful place to remember because of the many caring people who work there.

I've met the most beautiful people at the RAH. Patients, their families and all my beautiful nursing buddies.

Hard working and dedicated colleagues who are selfless and forever caring.

Going to miss the old, however it is time for the new.

Making lifelong friends that shared laughs and wonderful memories.

It has been a great opportunity working at the old RAH. I am very honoured to be a part of this historic moment to move from the old RAH to the new RAH.

Meeting all my wonderful work colleagues.

Great memories of a great place to work, great people, staff and patients.

Have loved working at the old RAH, looking from an admin and nurse perspective, great place to work and an awesome team we have here.

End of the oRAH, welcome nRAH.

It's all about the people and the care.

Great working environment, lots of memories to be remembered, thanks for the opportunities.

Proud to be a part of a working team in old RAH, and to the New RAH, all the best!

May the ghosts of the past protect you . . . you are the resting place.

Good memories of sending patients home.

So many shifts, specially one delivery man singing Pogues songs to me all night.

Saying goodbye to a favourite patient (who was palliative) knowing I wouldn't see him again.

Holding the hand of a man who had been in a car accident as he faced complete loss of vision.

The patients make this job worthwhile.

My first time treating a palliative patient and when she thanked me for what I was doing.

I remember working with great nurses in often difficult conditions, but excellent training. The patient was the most important thing in the hospital, which was told to us the first days of Preliminary Training School.

During my time the thing that stands out to me is the amazing endurance of humanity and those that keep trying to smile.

All of the wonderful nurses at the RAH male or female treated me very well.

Teaching spinal patients at the Hampstead how to paint. And get them to sing (Karaoke). I was an orderly there (30 years ago).

The wonderful care I received from the nursing staff, shared laughter and shared tears. Friendships formed. A nurse in spinal intensive care unit once burst a bag of IV Potassium that was hanging above her head, it was very funny.

Making the patient smile even though they're in pain.
It melts my heart that the little joke I have can make them happy.

Dr S saved my life in 1997.

I remember 30 years ago coming here for the first time. I went to the chest clinic then the cardiac clinic and Dr G diagnosed me with type 2 diabetes.

Thanks for your great care for my father and mother.

When I was looked after during my day surgery. Well done, happy memory.

Fond memories of my dear mum, who passed away in 2009.
She was looked after extremely well.

It may be old and grotty but so many patients have had lifesaving experiences here, so many amazing memories + friendships. Will miss you RAH!

Always having to wear the correct white coat, RAH revues, cricket matches against Flinders, opening the diabetes centre, the hole in the ground, which became the main building.

I have been a volunteer with the heritage unit for 5 years. It was a wonderful moment when I first saw 'Corporal Coles' hand'; Dr Florey's original penicillin growth. So many treasures we have.

On Sunday Myrna rang me; I had nursed Myrna 17 years ago. Over the 17 years we have sent a yearly Christmas card with the year's events written on the card. Last Christmas her card didn't arrive because Myrna was unwell. Sunday she called to wish me well for the big move to the new RAH. Feeling blessed to have met some special patients over the years. Those special ones like Myrna remain connected.

The small room in the nurse's station 'a little chill chat' place in burns unit will be missed.

Ringing the bell when visiting hours were over.

Blackout at the RAH once where no one knew what to do. Registrar: 'I had all these letters that I was going to dictate just this afternoon! What a shame.'

Indoor cricket, quiet radiology days.

It's all going to be great in nRAH. The lifts in East wing stop and start and don't open on time. When they did, it would sometimes be not level with the floor.

Finding my way to Medical Art and Design the first time was like an *Alice in Wonderland, Harry Potter, Being John Malkovich* or *Secret Squirrel* experience.

On New Year's Eve sending champagne through the tube system.

Going up to the helipad New Year's Eve and seeing the fireworks.

Ural in the men's bottles and short sheeting the beds of long-term, young patients.

Accidentally spilling the contents of a G&O and then proceeding to slip over in it was very embarrassing.

Cordial parties in S3 room post ortho huddle, lemon is the best!

1959. Matron H said: 'Always put your lipstick on; patients want you to look bright and cheery.'

Dancing in the storeroom after a hard shift with Emma!

Dancing in the storeroom after a hard shift with Jayne! #danceislife.

Tearoom chats with staff from your area about your area.

Having been asked to look after a 12 year old – his mother was a patient – my thoughts were what to do with him. I put him to work filling up blankets, tea and coffee, and picking up sandwiches. All the nursing staff were praising him. When a social worker spoke to him about being upset, he answered with no, it has been super cool. Yes, he loved all the attention from staff.

Surgical specialities, out-patient nurses' famous tea parties, all red food!

Our ward parties, teamwork, fun times, jokes, family.

A lasting memory of mine would definitely be the hand drawn map of the hospital I received on my first day. It was terrible, and I got lost multiple times in the first couple of weeks. I am ready for the new maze.

I met my now husband in the old RAH foyer in 2011, dressed in tinsel, singing Christmas carols for the med student orchestra. 2 and a half years married and comfy! Thanks old RAH!

Coming to visit grandparents as a child and riding the big escalator.

This was a great place for welcoming migrant working women.
My mother was trained as a cook in the metabolic ward.
A welcoming and professional place.

I won't forget having sinks and dryers next to our printers, and shavers above our filing cabinets and toilets with our storeroom files, as our office used to be a ward!

Water fights with saline syringes and 'POETS' days.

In the early 80s it was eerie walking on level 1 to use the vending machines, it felt haunted.

I loved the Christmas nativity parade with all the wise men and shepherds with the orderlies and others in costume. I will also miss the carols in the chapel afterwards.

Smoking outside B4.

Waiting forever for the lifts, fire alarms going off in the middle of the night waking all the patients, absconding patients being found by the police and returned to the ward.

Angela put ice cream in the vac chute and sent it and broke the machine.

I will never forget our delirious night shift memories.

The first day I arrived at the RAH was in 1961. My mother was in Hope ward with women's issues and walked out with a baby. It was a surprise for my mother and my family didn't know she was pregnant, nor is the old RAH a maternity hospital. Years later I came back to the old RAH to see the era out and the new chapter begin at the new RAH.

During August 1966, whilst working my first ever night shift in the Rhesus department, we decided that we would make a batch of marmalade as we were never that busy. Sister D brought in the citrus which was beautifully cut and left to soak during the day. Upon arrival to work the next night, we read a note advising us that we could complete the marmalade but we were not to make any more. The marmalade was made, put into jars and all staff helped themselves to a sample. Night shift in 1966 in Rhesus, i.e. blood transfusion, was always quiet but by 1969 had become quite a busy shift. The department was located upstairs from the McEwin theatres.

1981. I met my husband when he was a patient at the chest clinic and then on S2 when he was admitted as an inpatient. He was a Vietnamese refugee admitted with TB. His only family was a younger brother who was at school. The Vietnamese patients had trouble eating the hospital food, not being used to a western diet. As a TB nurse I knew the importance of nutrition for TB patients. As the daughter of a chef and a cook myself who loved Vietnamese food, I used to cook Vietnamese meals for our TB Vietnamese inpatients and bring them in from home. To thank me when he was better, he asked me for coffee, and from there our relationship progressed. I have the RAH to thank for our beautiful daughter.

Dear old RAH: My journey began in 2002; over the 15 years I have seen sadness & witnessed miracles, I have laughed & cried. I have worked with some of the most amazing doctors and nurses. I have made some lifetime friends. I will treasure the memories always. Goodbye old RAH.

Goodbye old RAH.

A picture is worth a thousand words . . . a building is worth a lifetime of memories.

Goodbye SA Pathology, no more ghosts, and no more long walks.

For three generations our family have walked these corridors as doctors, nurses and physiotherapists. Will miss feeling their presence in these old walls as I start a new walk down the road.

I have been to various hospitals in my working life but always come back to the RAH. It is like coming home in many ways. I trained here, met my wonderful wife here, and have been a patient here. No matter the building, it is the RAH family that matters.

Dear good old RAH. Thank you for the opportunity to serve her, looking forward to the nRAH to be of servitude to the public. We will not be taking the Grey Nurse though. Bye, bye and stay functional.

The RMO society and Jolly Bar, so many good memories!

The Jolly bar in all its many locations.

Friday evenings at the Jolly bar. A great place to relax.
Sad to see there is no equivalent at the new RAH.

Parking and chopper/air flights

Parking in the dirt paddock in the rain before the car park was built.

Flying around the state picking up critically ill patients.

Grey Nurse

5–6 am in the stairwell in East Wing and there were clinking of chains. Must have been the Grey Nurse!

Sitting on a stool in S5 getting told ghost stories by EN Ros.

16 September 1941, first day on duty at the RAH, now in 2017, still here, great memories.

Cardiac arrest in A4, and someone went around and reassured the patients. Who? The Grey Nurse.

I remember the Grey Nurse . . . I pretended to be her and scared nurses coming out of theatre.

The grey ghost of east wing.

The 80s were the best, lots of partying and camaraderie between the 'pinky' students. The pizza being sent through the wooden tube to your mates. The Botanic Hotel on a Monday night.

Fondly remembering all the 'pinkys'. The north wing level 2 kiosk and the many hundreds of patients and friends along the way. 28 years and counting. 13 to go at nRAH.

Dressed in candy stripes with my ice cream cone cap, with black stockings in 1971. I was barely 17 years old. Times have changed.

Group 882 dressed in pink. This place changed my life, thank you to all the wonderful educators.

After thirty plus years as a worker in the kitchen my co-workers are like family, we have had lots of happiness with weddings, birthdays and births, but also a lot of sadness with co-workers and family passing away. But altogether, lots of Happy Memories.

In the ward in the 1970s the kitchen staff would hand out drinks from a trolley for morning and afternoon tea. In winter, the trolley had large stainless-steel jugs full of thick hot vegetable soup, which was very popular with nurses and interns. I always associate the east wing with smell of vegetable soup.

I remember my first day, getting lost trying to find the kitchen, lots of new friends along the way, 10 years in the old RAH.

I have been working in the kitchen for 15 months and it has been the best job I have ever had.

Ah the Resi wing in the 1980s, fun, fun, with no sleep.

Staying in the Nurse's quarters in the Resi wing.

Residential wing was used for nurses, with 1 floor for males. We used to have male nights and parties in the 'male floor' lounge common rooms.

Used to sneak into the old nurses' quarters in the 1970s.

Fun in the Nurses' Home.

Best memory – it's 1978 and we sneak out of the nurses' quarters and head across the road to the Botanic.

I was lucky enough to be in the last year of RAH training in 1990. Straight out of high school, living in the residential wing for a few years. One of my classmates kept an orphaned joey kangaroo in a Sportsgirl bag in her room. We would take it out for a hop around in the botanic gardens. We loved to party in the south wing with DJ Panda on Monday nights at the Botanic hotel.

In loving memory of Tony and Brad of ward C3 in the RAH. RIP and thank you for the memories.

Rick and Ron, a couple of great nurses who are now in heaven. Please direct them to the new RAH.

A place where mental health was being taken care of. That of the patients and staff.

4 week loan, SS to P4BU with no green card.

I worked here for years and got a book.

Thank you for all the wonderful support you have given to our Cara customers over the years. Good luck for your relocation and enjoy the new RAH.

Dad did joinery for the radiotherapy building and I worked for the Baulderstone building. 15/66 – Dental Building. 23/66 North Wing Ward block. And others.

ED Dept – won't miss the days of 95 patients in the department.

I first worked in RAH as a locum in neurology. It was over summer and became very quiet. I was able to sit and watch Allan Border and Jeff Thomson fighting unsuccessfully to save the Boxing Day Test, sitting in an unoccupied patient lounge.

Arrival to Adelaide 2014.

I loved you from the moment I laid eyes on you. First place I worked with a bar.

Good memories = Beautiful Nurses! Bad memories = All forgotten! New and great beginnings are often disguised as painful memories.

Goodbye. Farewell. Amen.

Wakefield Press is an independent publishing and distribution company based in Adelaide, South Australia. We love good stories and publish beautiful books. To see our full range of books, please visit our website at www.wakefieldpress.com.au where all titles are available for purchase. To keep up with our latest releases, news and events, subscribe to our monthly newsletter.

Find us!

Facebook: www.facebook.com/wakefield.press
Twitter: www.twitter.com/wakefieldpress
Instagram: www.instagram.com/wakefieldpress